ATTENTION DEFICIT DISORDERS,

HYPERACTIVITY

AND ASSOCIATED DISORDERS

ATTENTION DEFICIT DISORDERS, HYPERACTIVITY AND ASSOCIATED DISORDERS

A Handbook For Parents and Professionals

FIFTH EDITION

March 1988

BY WENDY S. COLEMAN, M.D.

2115 Chadbourne Avenue
Madison, Wisconsin, 53705

ATTENTION DEFICIT DISORDERS, HYPERACTIVITY AND
ASSOCIATED DISORDERS

A *Handbook for Parents and Professionals*

FIFTH EDITION

1984 First Edition
1985 Second Edition
1986 Third Edition
1987 Fourth Edition
1988 Fifth Edition

International Standard Book Numbers:
ISBN 0-9620187-0-8 (Cloth)
ISBN 0-9620187-1-6 (Paper)
Library of Congress Catalog Card Number: 88-70410

Printed in the United States of America
Typesetting and production by Impressions, Inc.,
P.O. Box 3304, Madison, WI 53704
Cover design and calligraphy by Linda Hancock, Madison, Wisconsin

Published by:

2115 Chadbourne Avenue
Madison, Wisconsin
53705

CONTENTS

ACKNOWLEDGMENTS

Children with serious behavior problems are a challenge for parents, educators and health professionals. Hyperactivity and attention deficit disorders often accompany other medical and neurologic disorders. These children may need the help of different specialists in order to evaluate and care for their special needs and abilities.

The following information is presented in hopes that it will provide the knowledge that parents, educators and health professionals need to find the help these children deserve.

My sincere thanks go to the children and their families who have allowed me to share in their lives and to my own children who teach me daily. I am also grateful to the many teachers, social workers, psychologists and other health professionals for their participation in the evaluation and treatment of these children.

There are many people who helped with the fifth edition of this book. My special thanks go to my mother, Jean Steinhart, who edited much of the everchanging material and continues to provide me with life-long encouragement and love. Cheryl Schneller has given me feedback and suggestions for new material. Mike Pitterle assisted with computer problems and with the daily chores of my clinical practice, freeing some of my time for writing. My thanks go to Linda Hancock for her artistic creativeness and calligraphy.

I would like to thank especially all of my office staff who patiently put up with the stresses of my busy clinical practice and my overabundant energy.

If my son, Nick, had not persisted in our family's need for a computer, I might never have learned that I could write. Thanks also to Megan and Jennifer, my creative and hard-working daughters, AKA the mailroom staff.

Most of all, without the technical, editorial and moral support of my husband, this book would have remained only an idea. This book is my thanks to his caring and encouragement.

Wendy S. Coleman, M.D., F.A.A.P.
Jackson Clinic Pediatrics
345 West Washington Avenue
Madison, Wisconsin, 53703

DENNIS THE MENACE

1

Attention Deficit Disorders and Hyperactivity

What Is An "Attention Deficit Disorder"?

Attention deficit disorder (called ADD for short) is a term used to describe a set of symptoms many children share. ADD is not an illness or a disorder, but rather a group of characteristics found in many different children. Like any other symptom, ADD can be a mild, moderate or severe problem. The characteristics of ADD include short attention span, trouble concentrating, distractibility and poor impulse control. Hyperactivity may also be seen but not all children with ADD are hyperactive. Many professionals consider ADD to be a learning disability. Children with ADD may have significant behavior problems and may find it hard to work up to their ability in school.

What Is "Attending"?

At first glance, attending appears to be a simple concept. Researchers, however, have found that what we call "attending" is a complex process made up of different parts.

First, attention is dependent how interesting the material is and how it is presented. The more interesting the material, the more likely the child is to attend. The way in which material is presented will also affect the child's attention. A creative teacher who presents material in an exciting way will be more likely to capture and hold a child's attention than a teacher who presents the same information in a dull manner. Children with ADD continue to have problems paying attention even with a good teacher, but they may attend better if the material captures their interest.

A second component of attending has to do with the child's motivation. For most students, motivation improves when the material is interesting. There are occasional children who can not be motivated for any educational learning. These children have been "turned off" or "burned out." They may come from severely chaotic homes where there is little supervision and minimal value placed on learning. They may be children who have been chronically frustrated by inappropriate school placement, frequent moves, changes in schools, chronic illness, undiagnosed learning disabilities or many missed weeks of school. Children with ADD are motivated by material that interests them, but are unable to sustain attention despite this motivation. Some children with learning disabilities or ADD may appear to have good motivation at home and in the early years at school but lose motivation as they get into the later elementary grades and middle school. Long standing frustration, confusion, failure and unpredictability eventually dampen their motivation.

A third component of attending is the child's ability to tell the difference between important and unimportant material. For example, children should be able to read a paragraph and then identify the main ideas in it and then focus on this material.

A final component of attention is "vigilance" or the ability of the child to sustain attention and ignore other external or internal distractions. Other irrelevant sights, sounds and thoughts compete for and grab the child's attention. Children with ADD are unable to maintain vigilance and are easily distracted in most academic and in many home situations.

What Problems Do Children Have With Short Attention Span?

Children with ADD are unable to sustain their attention in most situations. Even when there are minimal distractions, the child's mind seems to go from one thought or activity to another. These children have difficulty finishing a sentence, following directions or completing school assignments. They will play with a toy for a few minutes and then something else will catch their attention. They usually are unable to stay with any activity for very long unless the activity gives them immediate feedback or is very interesting. These attending problems are not caused by lack of motivation.

Do Children Grow Out Of Their Attention Problems?

Occasionally, disorders in attending may be due to slow development. Infants and toddlers are expected to have very short attention spans. They loose interest in an activity after a few minutes and look for something new and different. By four years of age, most children are able to enjoy quiet time while a parent reads them a story. Kindergarten children can sit and listen for short periods and can engage in brief learning activities. Attention and concentration should mature as the child ages and develops. Children do not mature at the same rate. Some attend well at a very early age. Even as toddlers, they are able to focus and stay on task for long periods of time. Other children continue to have trouble attending until late in elementary school.

Disorders in attending may also be due to a malfunction that never corrects itself. These children have significant problems throughout their school years and into adulthood. They may learn skills to compensate for their disorder and may function very successfully despite their problems.

Or they may continue to struggle, avoiding tasks that require concentration and attention.

What Is Increased Distractibility?

Children who are distractible are unable to keep their attention focused. Their attention is drawn to things most of us ignore. They may have difficulty staying with any activity for more than a few minutes because of this distractibility. They are less apt to be distracted if they are involved in an activity they really like such as watching a favorite TV program. They also are less distracted when they are working one-to-one with a teacher or other adult. They may be well-behaved in the doctor's office or in other new situations. They are distracted mostly in a large group or in an unstructured situation. They have trouble concentrating on their school work or on other routine tasks that require their attention for long periods. Poor school performance despite good ability is a frequent reason these children are referred for professional help.

Parents and teachers often notice that children with ADD are unable to follow complex directions. The children start out with good intentions but are distracted quickly and forget what they are supposed to be doing. Problems with distractibility are part of the cause of this difficulty.

What Is "Poor Impulse Control"?

Children with poor impulse control are best described as "acting before they think" or "acting without considering the consequences." They need more adult supervision to keep them out of trouble than most children their age. In school, common complaints are that they talk out of turn, have trouble waiting, touch or hit other children, or say things that are inappropriate. Some children are impulsive in a physically aggressive way. They can't seem to keep their hands to themselves and hit or touch others inappropriately with minimal cause.

What Is "Hyperactivity"?

Children are active by their very nature. The hyperactive child is just a lot busier. Compared to the usual busy child, the hyperactive child rarely seems to stop. He (or she) is not just busy, but is unfocused or unorganized. Some hyperactive children have trouble getting to sleep or give up napping at an early age. Other hyperactive children need 12 hours of sleep at night and drop off to sleep the moment their heads touch the pillow. Some hyperactive preschoolers wake in the middle of the night full of energy, wanting to play or ransack the refrigerator. Hyperactive children are especially difficult to manage in situations where there is a lot of stimulation or activity. Their hyperactivity worsens when there is more activity around them and when they are tired.

Almost but not all children who are hyperactive have attention deficits. Not all children who have ADD are hyperactive.

Children who have ADD and who are hyperactive may mature out of the hyperactivity as they get older. This usually happens in the early teen years. It is not clear why this occurs in some children and not in others. A child who is hyperactive and has ADD may outgrow the hyperactivity but continue to have the attention problems through the teen years and into adulthood.

How Common Is ADD?

The figures for this vary depending on how ADD is defined but most experts feel that one child in every 20 to 50 children has ADD.

Attention problems range from being mild to very severe. Hyperactive children who have ADD are more likely to come to the attention of a professional because the hyperactivity is so noticeable. According to research studies, boys are six times more likely than girls to be hyperactive and to have attention deficits. Girls are more likely to have the attention deficits without the hyperactivity. Girls with ADD may be well-behaved, and therefor less likely to come to the attention of school personnel even though their school performance may suffer significantly.

Do Children Outgrow ADD And Hyperactivity?

The process of growth and maturation continues from infancy into adulthood. Some ADD children seem to take longer to develop age-appropriate attention and concentration abilities. Some develop adequate skills in this area at a much older age than other children. They are delayed in maturing in this area. Other ADD children seem to have disordered attention and concentration abilities that continue unchanged through their teen years and into adulthood.

Children with maturational attention problems are likely to begin to improve during the teen years. Other children learn how to work around their problems and develop strategies to successfully manage difficult situations. After the completion of high school, there is greater freedom of choice and flexibility for most people. Teens and adults with ADD are more likely to choose areas of work that allow their strengths to develop.

Are There Other Characteristics That Are Also Seen In Children With ADD?

Children with ADD are often described as stubborn, negative, depressed, disorganized, immature socially and emotionally, easily frustrated, clumsy, aggressive and resistant to discipline. They may be happy, energetic, creative, socially comfortable and oblivious to their problems. Children with ADD may also be enuretic (bed-wetting at night after the age of five years) and have problems with stool soiling. Speech problems, developmental delays and learning disabilities are also frequently seen in these children. Each child is unique and may have some, none or all of these additional characteristics.

Why Do ADD Children Behave Normally At Times?

Many children with ADD will behave better in certain situations. This change in behavior can be very confusing for parents, teachers and physicians. Fathers (or significant men in the family) may have less trouble managing ADD children than mothers. Children with ADD may have a "honeymoon" period of good behavior when they start a new year in school. They may be well-behaved in the doctor's office. Babysitters and grandparents may have less of a problem managing them. Situations that provide immediate feedback, such as video games and computers, often hold the attention of these children for longer periods.

How Is ADD Diagnosed?

Unfortunately there is no blood or psychological test for ADD. Since many children have some of the characteristics of ADD, it may be difficult to decide when the problems are severe enough to warrant evaluation and treatment. The decision to treat a child should be made after a careful and thorough evaluation. (See chapter on evaluating ADD children). Parents, school teachers, psychologists and social workers are a very important source of information during both the evaluation and treatment process. An evaluation for ADD should be done by a specialist who is familiar with children and these problems. School personnel may be knowledgeable about ADD and may suggest that a child needs further evaluation.

It is important for parents to remember that hyperactive children may behave normally while seeing their regular physician for check-ups. Parents may ask the physician during a visit if their child is hyperactive. The physician may say, based on a limited sample of time with the child, that the child does not appear to have a problem. Because many hyperactive children behave normally in a quiet, restrictive environment, this is not an adequate place to assess a child. If there is a question about ADD, a full evaluation should be undertaken by a well-trained professional.

SUGGESTED READINGS ABOUT ATTENTION DEFICIT DISORDERS

Diagnostic And Statistical Manual Of Mental Disorders, (3rd Edition). American Psychiatric Association: 1980, 475 pages. Paperback. About $10.00. This manual describes the criteria that mental health professionals use in assigning diagnostic categories for disorders that affect behavior, mood and conduct in adults and children. Most of the material in the book relates to adult disorders. About 100 pages deal with childhood disorders including attention deficit disorders, affective disorders, conduct disorders and Tourette's syndrome.

Barkley, Russell. *Hyperactive Children, A Handbook For Diagnosis And Treatment.* New York: Guilford Press. 1980. Hard cover. 458 pages. About $30.00. This is an excellent text book meant for professionals who work with attention deficit disorder and hyperactive children. The chapters on behavior management are excellent and may be of interest to parents willing to tackle the 150 pages.

Wender and Wender. *The Hyperactive Child And The Learning Disabled Child.* Crown Press. 1978. About $10.00. 134 pages. This is a very well-written guide for parents and health professionals. Chapter headings include: characteristics of children with hyperactivity, causes, outcome and treatment of hyperactive children and learning disabilities.

Woodward, Dan and Norma Biondo. *Living Around The Now Child.* Columbus, Ohio: Merrill Publishing. 1972. Paperback. 125 pages. About $11.00. This excellent book describes and makes understandable the many frustrating behaviors of children with learning disabilities and attention deficits. Understanding why these children need so much help to get a task done, or to get through the day, makes the job of a parent or teacher less frustrating. This little book goes a long way in helping parents and educators to work together to give "Now" children the best possible chance for success.

2

The Causes of Attention Deficit Disorder

The term, attention deficit disorder, describes a collection of symptoms. Like other symptoms, (fever is a good example), there are many causes of attention problems. ADD can be inherited in a family, just like eye color or allergy. It can also be acquired in infancy and childhood from various injuries or illnesses.

The more common causes of ADD have been grouped below into general categories. As more is learned about this group of disorders, additional causes may be found. The majority of children referred for evaluation of attention problems will have primary attention deficit disorders. Of the children with secondary attention deficits, most will have associated disorders of mood and behavior. The other secondary causes of ADD are less common but not rare.

Primary Attention Deficit Disorders

Primary disorders may occur with or without hyperactivity, learning disabilities, or developmental delays. Primary ADD is usually inherited.

Secondary Attention Deficit Disorders

Secondary disorders may occur as part of the expression of another primary illness or injury.

1. Associated with other disorders of mood and behavior such as affective disorders or schizophrenia
2. Associated with primary neurologic disorders such as Tourette's syndrome, Neurocutaneous disorders or epilepsy
3. Associated with chromosomal disorders such as Fragile X syndrome
4. Caused by injury to the developing fetus from infection, trauma, stress or hypoxia
5. Injury to the child from toxins, infection, severe brain damage due to an accident, or exposure to radiation for the treatment of brain tumors or childhood leukemia

The clinical descriptions given in the following sections are based on the histories and experiences of many hundreds of ADD children. They are presented to give a sample of the variety of problems these children exhibit.

PRIMARY ATTENTION DEFICIT DISORDERS

Primary Attention Deficit Disorder With Hyperactivity

John was well-known to his pediatrician. Within minutes of his arrival in the office, everyone knew that John was there. He was only five years old, but had the activity level of four children. The doctor had to keep an eye on the supplies in the exam room. John was up on the desk, checking out the tongue blades the moment the doctor turned to wash her hands in the sink. John's mother had jokingly mentioned that she considered buying a harness with a leash when John was two years old for shopping excursions. He actually had gotten lost twice in the shopping center. When he was eight months old, he unexpectedly climbed out of his crib. From the time he could walk, he was into everything. John was about to enter kindergarten and the pediatrician suggested that John be watched carefully for attention problems as he started school.

Primary Attention Deficit Disorder With An Associated Learning Disorder

Patty had been in a class for children with learning disabilities since first grade. She was a quiet child who had difficulty with reading and math skills. Her first and second grade teachers were concerned with her ability to stay on task and her impulsivity. In the small learning disabilities class, the teacher had been able to redirect her attention with frequent reminders and extra help. The third grade LD teacher noticed that Patty's attention problems were having more impact on her progress. Patty was particularly frustrated by her home work. Her mother knew it took her longer than the other children to finish her work because of the distractibility. Patty began to talk about how "stupid" she was.

Dick had been evaluated by the school's multidisciplinary team when he was 8 years old. His teachers described him as a very caring and creative child. He had a very severe expressive language problem that made it difficult to understand what he was trying to say. He would start a sentence with a good idea and then would loose his train of thought. Most of the time the teacher and his classmates had to struggle to understand him. *He was impulsive, distractible and had trouble finishing his work. If his teacher sat with him, or stood near him to keep him on task, he did much better. If the teacher left him alone, he would rarely finish his assignments. He called out answers without waiting for his turn. His classmates teased him because he "sounded funny" to them. His teacher discovered that Dick expressed himself with pictures more clearly than he could with words. Testing and observation revealed that Dick was intellectually gifted in many areas but had a severe problem with expressive language, attention, concentration and distractibility. His uncle and a nephew had similar problems with expressive language and attention. The school "M" team recommended special help for the expressive language problems, inclusion in activities for gifted children, and a referral for assessment and treatment of his attention deficit disorder.*

Primary Attention Deficit Disorder With Developmental Delay

Robert finally learned to read at the end of third grade. He had received special help in school since kindergarten. His handwriting was difficult to read, but he was showing improvement as he practiced writing in "cursive." As a baby, his motor development had been slow. He sat at 8 months, crawled at 12 months and walked at twenty months. He had received help for speech and expressive language problems until second grade. His teachers and his parents had been concerned about his attention, concentration and impulsivity since kindergarten. He had started taking stimulant medication in first grade. His parents and his teachers had seen a dramatic improvement. Robert told his doctor that the medication helped him control his body and that he didn't get into trouble in school like he did before. He was proud of his progress and achievements. After he finished his first quarter in sixth grade, his physician suggested that he stop the stimulant medication. Robert's progress would be watched carefully. The physician was hoping that Robert's ability to attend and concentrate had matured just as his reading, speech and language skills and coordination had improved over the past few years.

SECONDARY ATTENTION DEFICIT DISORDERS

Secondary Attention Deficit Disorder
Associated With Affective Disorder

Steve had been treated with stimulant medication for several years for his attention deficit disorder. He was a very gifted child and his ability to concentrate and attend in school had improved significantly with the medication. Despite this improvement, his parents continued to worry about his irritability and sullen mood. He would get angry without any reason. Things had to be just right or he screamed, kicked, and threw things in his room. At school, he was withdrawn and refused to do work unless it interested him. His teacher described him as depressed and angry at the same time. At home his frequent, unprovoked outbursts disrupted the entire family. A detailed family history revealed that several of his father's relatives had been treated for serious depressive episodes. Two relatives had attempted suicide. Steve's mood improved dramatically with the addition of a tricyclic at bedtime. He continued to take his stimulant medication for the attention problems. His sleep improved as well when the tricyclic medication was started. His teacher now complimented Steve regularly on his cooperative attitude, creativity and fine work.

Secondary Attention Deficit Disorder Associated With Neurologic Problems

TOURETTE'S SYNDROME—This is a disorder characterized by motor and vocal tics. It is often inherited and may be first noticed in children as young as four to six years old. This disorder is much more common in boys than girls. About 60% of children with Tourette's syndrome also have attention deficit disorders. The kinds of tics these children have vary. Some children have vocal tics (repeated clearing of the throat, animal noises, swearing under their breath) and others have motor tics (a repeated muscle twitch or jerk). The type of tic or its location may change after a few days or weeks. Although most children with Tourette's syndrome can control the tics for brief periods, this is an involuntary nervous disorder and should be treated medically.

Bill had been treated for the past year with stimulant medication for distractibility, impulsiveness and hyperactivity. His teachers and parents were pleased with his progress in school. Prior to starting the medication his parents had noticed that he would occasionally twitch his neck and shoulders. The twitching would go away after several weeks and then would return. His parents thought this was a nervous habit. Bill's grandfather had a similar twitch for most of his life. Bill's teacher became concerned when Bill began making noises in the classroom. The noises sounded like Bill was trying to clear his throat. Later they sounded more like grunts or animal noises. Bill didn't seem to be aware that he was making the noises. The diagnosis of Tourette's syndrome was confirmed by Bill's pediatrician.

The stimulant medication was stopped and a tricyclic was used to help with the attention problems. The motor and vocal tics were noticeable only occasionally.

NEUROCUTANEOUS DISORDERS—These are disorders of various parts of the body including the nervous system and skin. Tuberous Sclerosis and Neurofibromatosis are the medical terms for these disorders. Children develop many dark or light patches of skin. Some, but not all of these children have attention and learning problems, mild retardation, seizures and other medical problems.

Jeff and his mother had just moved from another state. Jeff needed a current physical examination to enroll in his new school. He had been evaluated and treated by a psychiatrist for hyperactivity and attention problems in the past but had not had a physical examination for many years. Records were requested from the previous psychiatrist which documented successful treatment with stimulant medication. The pediatrician immediately noticed many irregularly shaped areas of increased skin pigmentation on Jeff's chest, back and legs when he was examined. X-Rays of the spine were obtained to check for neurofibromas involving the spinal roots. Jeff's hearing was tested because of the incidence of tumors that impair hearing. Jeff and his mother were given information about neurofibromatosis and the national neurofibromatosis foundation.

WILLIAMS SYNDROME—This disorder causes autistic-like behavior in young children who also have unusual facial features and heart problems. Williams syndrome is very rare and symptoms appear by two years of age in most affected children. Children with Williams syndrome may also have problems with attention, concentration and impulsivity.

SEIZURE DISORDERS—Some children with epilepsy will also have attention deficit disorders.

Sue began having generalized seizures when she was two years old. Her first seizure occurred when she had a high fever due to a viral infection. The seizure lasted 4 minutes. The family doctor examined her carefully and reassured her parents that the fever was probably the cause of the seizure. No treatment was prescribed at that time. Sue's mother noticed another brief seizure six months later when she had no illness at all. She called her doctor right away. At that time, Sue was examined by her doctor and by a neurologist. An EEG and additional blood tests were ordered by the neurologist. The EEG was abnormal and the neurologist prescribed medication to con-

trol the seizures. Sue had a third seizure when she was four years old. A blood test indicated that the dose of medication was too low to effectively prevent seizures. The dose of medication was increased and she had no further seizures. Sue began to have trouble with her school work in third grade. She worked hard and her parents knew it took her longer to complete her home work than other children. Her teachers always described her as a very pleasant, quiet child who needed to be reminded to stay on task. They often found her playing with things at her desk or looking out the window when she should be working. The neurologist asked for more information from Sue's current teacher and from her past teachers. The teachers all found Sue to be a lovely, cooperative child who tried hard. They all agreed that she was distractible, inattentive and impulsive. A recent evaluation by the school psychologist confirmed that Sue had average academic abilities but was more than a grade behind in her academic skills. The neurologist discussed treatment for ADD with Sue and her mother.

Secondary Attention Deficit Disorder
Associated With Chromosomal Abnormalities

FRAGILE X SYNDROME—This is a relatively common cause of mild to severe retardation and is more common in boys than girls. Boys are affected more severely than girls. Adolescent boys with this syndrome may have large testicles but their physical features are otherwise normal. This syndrome was first recognized in 1975. Children, especially boys with ADD who have mild to severe retardation and a family history of another similarly affected male, should be tested for fragile X syndrome.

John had been in an early childhood program since his third birthday. His kindergarten teacher was concerned about his hyperactivity, distractibility and impulsiveness. She doubted that he would be ready academically for first grade in the fall. He still couldn't recognize all of the letters of the alphabet. His mother reported that his kindergarten physical examination had been normal. A careful family history revealed that several other males on his mother's side of the family had been in special education classes and had also had behavior problems. Testing by the school psychologist revealed that John had academic abilities in the higher end of the educable retarded range. Chromosome testing confirmed that John and several of his family had fragile X syndrome. His mother also carried the fragile X chromosome but had no clinical evidence of the disorder.

Secondary Attention Deficit Disorders Due To Fetal Injury

FETAL DILANTIN COMPLEX—Exposure to Dilantin and other medications given to pregnant women to control seizures may cause ADD and other distinctive physical abnormalities. Not all babies exposed to Dilantin will be born with ADD or physical problems. There appear be other unknown factors that cause certain babies to be susceptible to damage from these medications.

FETAL ALCOHOL SYNDROME—Alcohol taken by the mother during pregnancy, especially during the first three months of gestation, can severely damage the unborn child. Children born with fetal alcohol syndrome are very short, have small heads and have a group of distinctive physical and developmental abnormalities.

> *Robin was adopted when she was two weeks old. Her mother had terminated her parental rights shortly after birth because she was not particularly interested in the baby. She had not been aware of her pregnancy until the fifth month and had only come to the clinic for prenatal care 10 weeks before the delivery. She admitted that she had a problem with alcohol and had not changed her drinking habits during the pregnancy. Robin was very small at birth, although the doctors felt she was a term baby. As she grew older, her weight, height and head circumference continued to be below the 3rd percentile for her age. Her pediatrician confirmed that she had many of the features seen in children with fetal alcohol syndrome. Her hyperactivity and attention problems were noticed during the first year of life and continued to be a problem in the early childhood program she started at 3 years of age.*

EXPOSURE TO HEROIN AND OTHER ABUSIVE DRUGS—Other abusive drugs (heroin, cocaine, speed, etc.) taken by the mother during pregnancy may cause damage to the developing brain of the baby and potentially can cause ADD.

PRENATAL INFECTION—Infection in the unborn baby from cytomegalic inclusion virus (CMV) or toxoplasmosis. Both of these unusual infections cause injury to the brain and other organs of unborn babies while causing minimal illness in the pregnant mother. These babies may have physical abnormalities and trouble gaining weight during the first year of life.

> *Cindy had been hospitalized as an infant because of persistent vomiting and failure to gain weight. She had been a very small baby but had not gained weight adequately. Her physical examination on*

admission to the hospital also showed an enlarged liver and spleen. Pyloric stenosis was diagnosed by X-Ray soon after she was admitted. During surgery to correct the pyloric stenosis, the surgeon had taken a biopsy of the enlarged liver. Cindy's vomiting stopped after the surgery and she slowly began to gain weight. The liver biopsy and then a urine test confirmed that Cindy had been infected with cytomegalic inclusion virus. Several years later she was still below the 3rd percentile for height, weight and head circumference. She was enrolled in an early childhood program at three years of age. Her problems with attention, concentration and distractibility and learning were significant enough to delay entry into kindergarten until she was six years old. A referral was made because of possible ADD the following year.

CHRONIC HYPOXIA—Long-standing lack of oxygen to the developing baby during pregnancy. Unborn babies totally depend on the mother's placenta and the umbilical cord for oxygen, nutritional and metabolic needs. The placenta is subject to injury and improper development just like any other organ of the body.

SUDDEN OR ACUTE HYPOXIA—Sudden lack of oxygen during pregnancy, labor or delivery. There are several sudden complications of labor and delivery that may seriously threaten the baby's oxygen supply. The placenta may separate suddenly from the wall of the uterus before the baby is delivered. The umbilical cord may prolapse or be delivered before the baby's head. There may be unexpected problems delivering the head of a breech baby. Babies may have unanticipated malformations which complicate labor and delivery. Fortunately, these situations are uncommon. Newborn babies are unusually tolerant of stress and the hazards of birth. Children who are severely stressed at birth generally continue to have significant problems in the first days or weeks of life with breathing, feeding and movement.

Mary was born unexpectedly about a month early. Her mother was shopping when she felt an uncomfortable sensation. By the time she got to the hospital, she knew something was very wrong. The nurses and doctors on the OB floor worked as quickly as possible. Mary was born by Cesarean section within a very short time. Mary's mother had felt her membranes rupture suddenly and the cord that attached Mary to her placenta had slipped out of her mother's vagina. The doctors were not sure that Mary would be born alive. At the delivery Mary was blue and limp and there was a very faint heart beat. She needed the help of a respirator for several hours before she could breathe on her own. She was fed with a tube for two weeks before she was able to nurse adequately. Her development was delayed slightly but by four years of age she seemed like a happy, active little girl. Her early childhood teacher had suggested that she be evaluated for attention deficit disorder because it was almost impossible for her to concentrate, attend and focus on any activity. Her problems with language, speech and motor skills seemed less significant than her problems attending and concentrating.

PREMATURITY—In very premature babies (those who weigh under two pounds at birth). Since the early 1980's more very premature babies are surviving as a result of greatly improved intensive care. Some of these babies have serious medical problems because of their prematurity. Researchers are finding that as these babies mature, a significant number of them show learning problems and attention deficits.

Secondary Attention Deficit Due to Injury To The Brain In Childhood

EXPOSURE TO TOXINS—Exposure to lead and other heavy metals will cause significant brain damage. Young children may chew on window sills and crib railings. Lead used to be an ingredient in inexpensive paint. When the hazards of lead-based paint were discovered, this type of paint was removed from the market. In very old homes, especially in poorer urban neighborhoods, lead based paint may still be found.

SEVERE INFECTION INVOLVING THE BRAIN—Complication of Bacterial Meningitis or Severe Viral Encephalitis - Many children recover from meningitis or encephalitis completely. Severe infections can cause permanent damage in some children. ADD is one of many problems that can result.

Kate was a very happy and energetic second grader. Her hyperactivity, impulsiveness and distractibility had been a problem during first grade but her mother was told that she would grow out of it. Her second grade teacher was concerned because Kate was now in the lowest reading and math group. Unless something changed, Kate would have to repeat second grade. Her second grade teacher felt that she could do the work if she could keep her mind on it. Her distractibility and lack of concentration were beginning to interfere with her academic progress. Kate had been a "handful" since she learned to crawl. Her mother had to watch her constantly. She rarely sat still long enough for her mother to read her a book, and would only play with something for a few minutes before moving on to something else. Summertime was easier because Kate loved to play outside in the large enclosed yard. Kate was clumsy and often tripped or fell and hurt herself. She had broken her arm once when she fell off a low wall. She had also been very sick with bacterial meningitis when she was 3 months old. She had been so sick that her mother was afraid she might die. Kate had been brought to the hospital when her mother realized she had a high fever. Her temperature was 104.6 in the hospital. She was limp and unresponsive for two days. She needed intravenous feedings for almost a week and antibiotics for two weeks. By the fourth hospital day, her fever was lower and she began to move around and suck weakly. The doctors had been concerned about Kate's hearing and about future problems with learning and coordination. Her hearing was tested before she left the hospital and was fine. As she got older and learned to walk and talk, her mother stopped worrying about her development. The family had moved to a new town before Kate started kindergarten and their current doctor was unaware of the history of meningitis until Kate's mother asked about it at a physical exam the school requested. The pediatrician reminded Kate's mother that the problems Kate was having in school probably were related to the serious illness she had had. The pediatrician asked if other family members had problems with learning or attention and concentration. Kate's mother was sure that no one in either her family or Kate's father's family had had any problems like Kate's.

COMPLICATION OF SEVERE BRAIN INJURY—Severe head injury with prolonged periods of unconsciousness and injury to the brain itself can cause permanent brain damage. The residual from this kind of injury will depend on what part of the brain was injured, the degree of injury and how much the body is able to heal itself.

Robert was a very active 4th grade student. School work was easy for him and his grades and comments from his teacher were always very good. He loved being outside. He and his close friend down the street often would ride bikes together after school. One afternoon, just as it was beginning to get dark, the boys were riding home on their bikes when Robert was hit by a car. He was thrown in the air for some distance and hit the pavement. He was taken by ambulance to the local hospital. The doctors found that he had a severe concussion and a broken right arm and leg. Robert was unresponsive for 3 days. When he regained consciousness, he was unable to speak. He could point to what he wanted and shake his head to respond to questions. His speech gradually returned while he was in the hospital. For the six months following the accident, Robert continued to have some trouble finding the words he wanted to express himself. He also had trouble with remembering, concentrating and paying attention. Two years after the accident, the speech problems were hardly noticeable, but the memory problems and attention problems continued to interfere with his school work.

INJURY CAUSED BY EXPOSURE TO CRANIAL RADIATION—Radiation therapy is a very important treatment modality for children with leukemia and certain brain tumors. Some of these children, especially those who receive large doses of radiation to the brain, may develop problems including delayed sexual maturation, short stature, learning and attention problems.

Carrie had been diagnosed with acute lymphocytic leukemia when she was 4 years old. Her leukemia went into remission after a two year treatment program of chemotherapy and radiation to her head. Despite this treatment, which is effective in the majority of children with this form of leukemia, her disease returned. This time, the leukemia was only found within her central nervous system. She was treated with additional radiation to the head and spine and another three year course of chemotherapy. Her leukemia continues to be in remission After the second course of treatment her teachers began to notice that she had trouble remembering certain kinds of information. She had difficulty concentrating and was impulsive, distractible and fidgety. Testing also showed a significant learning disability.

Can Children Have More Than One Possible Cause Of ADD?

Some children can have several compounding problems, each of which alone might be the cause of ADD. Unfortunately it may be impossible to sort out how much each problem contributes to the child's difficulty. All problems must be addressed and treated to ensure the best possible outcome for the child.

Sue had been in her current foster home for the past three years. The current foster family planned to adopt Sue within the year. Sue's mother was well known to the social service agency because of chronic problems with alcohol and Sue showed many of the features of fetal alcohol syndrome. Sue had been removed from her mother's care when she was 3½ years old after a report of physical abuse by the mother's boyfriend. Sue's mother also had a history of recurrent, severe depression and had attempted suicide on two occasions. She had refused to follow suggested treatment plans after discharge from the hospital. Sue had been placed in foster care each time her mother had been hospitalized. Her problems with attention, concentration and impulse control were clear to all her teachers, but her periods of anger and outbursts and underlying sadness were harder to figure out. Her therapist felt that the mood problems could be explained by the chronic abuse and neglect but because of the significant family history of depression, she referred Sue to a child psychiatrist for evaluation of possible affective disorder. Sue's mood and behavior improved significantly with the addition of a tricyclic. She could work more effectively with her therapist on issues involving her past, and was gradually able to risk some attachment to her adoptive family.

3

Causes of Inattention, Distractibility and Impulsiveness that are not Attention Deficit Disorders

Children can have problems with attention, concentration and impulsivity and not have an attention deficit disorder. The following are examples of environmental or medical problems that may cause poor school performance, difficulty with attention, concentration and/or impulsive behavior. A thorough evaluation should identify these children so that they can be treated appropriately.

Lack Of Motivation

Some children have no interest in school work and do not gain any satisfaction from achieving in a school setting. Usually these children come from homes where school achievement is not valued. They may be so far behind academically that they feel overwhelmed. Some of these children have significant learning disabilities that have been chronically frustrating and handicapping. They may have failed for so long that that they no longer care. These children may amuse themselves with behavior that is disruptive and inattentive.

Even in the class for children with emotional disturbances, Dick was a challenge. He was constantly interrupting, getting out of his seat to bother another child, and fidgeting with his pencil when he did sit down. He finished assignments only when his teacher was sitting with him. He was absent from school at least once a week. A recent multidisciplinary team report indicated that the longest he had stayed in any one school was nine months. Dick told his classmates that he had to stay home from school to take care of his ailing mother. The school social worker tried unsuccessfully to contact Dick's mother to arrange a conference by mail and by phone. The social worker finally made a visit to his mother at her apartment. Dick's mother appeared to have very little interest in her son's academic progress. She was pleased that he stayed out of trouble and left her alone. The social worker felt there was reason to suspect that Dick's mother had a serious alcohol problem. The county social service agency was contacted and they began an assessment of the quality of Dick's home environment.

Boredom

Some children are so advanced academically that the work of the average classroom is of no interest to them. These children become motivated when learning is exciting and challenging. Usually teachers are able to identify these unusually gifted children. Gifted children may also have learning problems that make it more difficult for them to achieve in the classroom. The potential of some learning disabled children may not be appreciated even by an experienced teacher. Testing should identify these children.

Joe was a very shy, clumsy child who had just moved to town. This was his teacher's first year out of school and she was excited about getting to know her class of first graders. The other children in the class quickly recognized that Joe was different. He talked endlessly without ever getting to the point, and seemed to struggle to get his ideas out in words. He pouted and muttered when he was frustrated. He managed to complete some of his work but he often would stare out the window or draw cartoon figures on his paper. His teacher had to remind him constantly to pay attention to his work or to her directions. His academic progress was about average but his parents felt he was capable of doing much better work. He was eventually referred for testing. The teacher was surprised to find that he was an extremely bright child with a severe expressive language problem.

Physical And Sexual Abuse

After the onset of abuse, children can have sudden and striking behavioral changes. Problems with attention or hyperactivity may be seen in these children.

Paula was an average student. She was well-liked by her teachers and her classmates. Her teacher became very concerned because of the abrupt change in her behavior when she returned from spring vacation. She was unable to sit still and constantly called out of turn. Her concentration and attention were almost non-existent. The teacher called Paula's mother. She was concerned too because Paula seemed to be so withdrawn at home. Paula's mother talked with Paula at length when she returned home from school later in the day. Paula eventually confided to her mother that a new baby-sitter at her grand-mother's house had repeatedly molested her and threatened to hurt her grandmother if she told. Paula's mother contacted the local police. Arrangements were made for Paula and her parents to talk with a skilled therapist immediately.

Hyperthyroidism

In this condition, the thyroid gland becomes overactive and produces more thyroid hormone than the body needs. This is an uncommon cause of hyperactivity and behavioral problems in children. These children are often tall and have a noticeable goiter (enlargement of the thyroid gland). Girls are affected more frequently than boys. The usual time between the onset of symptoms and diagnosis of this problem is from six to twelve months. Children may be very active, restless, inattentive, irritable, moody and easily excitable. Tremor of the fingers may be noticed. Children may have had recent weight loss despite good appetites. Children who are suspected of having an abnormality of the thyroid gland should have appropriate blood tests to check the level of thyroid hormone.

Hirschprung's Disease

This is a bowel problem caused by lack of nerve endings in part of the large intestine. Usually the longer the interval between bowel movements (4–10 days), the more irritable and fidgety the child becomes. Children with this abnormality have bowel problems in the newborn period that continue until the disorder is corrected. Most of the children with Hirschprung's will be diagnosed and treated within the first few weeks of life. Rarely a child will have bowel difficulties for several years before this condition is identified. Treatment is to surgically remove the section of bowel that has no nerve endings and reconnect the normal bowel.

Peter's teacher was confused by his behavior in her first grade classroom. Most days she was sure he was hyperactive. He was irritable, distractible and very fidgety. He bothered other children and rarely finished his assignments but there were other days when he was pleasant, able to concentrate on his work and keep his hands to himself. The physician who examined Peter also took a careful history. Peter had never had a bowel movement without some kind of help. When he was an infant, his mother used suppositories to help him. He would go up to seven days without having a bowel movement. His mother had also noticed that his mood and behavior were much better for a few days after he had a bowel movement and then he would get more and more irritable until he was able to pass a stool again. A 37 year old uncle had had similar problems. Peter's mother assumed this was just the way Peter was. A rectal biopsy (done under local anesthesia in the doctor's office) confirmed the diagnosis of Hirschprung's disease and Peter had surgery to correct the condition. His problems at school vanished.

Chronic Lack Of Sleep Or Inadequate Nutrition

Children who are chronically sleep deprived or who are significantly malnourished may have trouble concentrating and may be easily distractible. These children are usually sluggish and irritable. Their behavior may improve significantly after eating breakfast or lunch provided by the school.

Family Stress and Violence

Children who witness violence at home or who are the object of bitter custody battles may be so emotionally conflicted that they are unable to focus their attention on school work. They may be withdrawn, hostile, anxious, distracted, impulsive, sad or overly anxious to please.

Atypical Seizure Disorders, Petit Mal Seizures

Atypical seizures may be very hard to recognize in young children. Psychomotor seizures may mimic purposeful, complicated although inappropriate motor acts. Temporal lobe seizures may look like periods of rage or explosive behavior. The child may seem totally out of control but alert and aware. Children with petit mal seizures have very short periods (3 to 30 seconds) when their thinking is disrupted by seizure activity. The child appears to be looking blankly at nothing in particular and has no memory for the short duration of the seizure. This condition is diagnosed with an EEG (Electroencephalogram). Some children must be "sleep deprived" in order for the EEG to show the seizure abnormality.

> *Peter had trouble concentrating and attending in school. He was a very cooperative and motivated child but was falling behind in his work because he rarely finished his assignments. He was never impulsive or a behavior problem in school. His mother had restricted his bike riding because while riding along the sidewalk, he and the bike would "keel over" as if he were no longer in control of himself and the bike. An EEG confirmed the fact that he was having petit mal seizures.*

4

Treatment of Attention Deficit Disorders and Hyperactivity

The treatment plan must be individualized or tailor-made for each child and family. In some situations the entire evaluation and treatment process can be handled by a single professional. For more complicated children, several professionals may need to be involved. Coordination and communication between the family, school and other professionals is an important part of the evaluation and treatment process. One professional should take responsibility as "case manager" for the child and family.

Parents with difficult children often blame themselves for their children's behavioral problems. They worry that they have been too strict, too relaxed, too distant, too nice, too inconsistent or "too" something else. Whatever they have done, they are somehow responsible for the problems the child is having. This is made worse by well-meaning grandparents, professionals, friends or teachers who may misunderstand and over-simplify the child's problem. Children with attention problems are temperamentally and neurologically different from other children. These children can be difficult to manage in the most skilled and patient families. With proper treatment these children are better able to respond to more usual management techniques.

Although the specific treatment plan will vary from one child to another, there are some general guidelines.

Information and Advocacy

Parents, family members, and other professionals (social workers, physical therapists), and school personnel must be informed about the nature of the child's problems and the specifics of the treatment plan. Many parents have had the experience of being blamed for their children's difficulties. Blame has no place in the treatment of these children. Parents, educators and health professionals must work together to develop the best possible coordinated treatment program for each child.

Parents are frequently frustrated because they must continually educate other people about their child's problems. Teachers may choose to approach each new class of children with a fresh look. Material in a child's school file may not be transferred when a child changes schools, even within the same school district. At the start of the year, some teachers need to be encouraged to thoroughly review old material about a complicated or unusual child. Advocacy and education are vitally important for each child and family with learning and behavioral problems. Knowledgeable parents and professionals can be very effective in helping to get the best care for difficult children. Parent support groups provide an invaluable resource for these families, their children and their communities. These groups provide educational programs, lending libraries and a comfortable atmosphere for sharing frustrations and successes. Parent support groups have been able to put pressure on governmental agencies to provide better funding for programs for their children. (See section on "Resources" for more information).

Attention to Physical Problems and Health

Behavior deteriorates in almost all children when they are sick. Children with behavioral problems and ADD may be less aware of their own physical discomfort and may not complain until they have a severe ear infection or sore throat. Early treatment of these problems is wise. Attention to other health needs such as hearing, vision or motor problems is important. The child's Pediatrician or Family Doctor should be comfortable working with difficult children and with the other health professionals involved in the child's treatment.

Attention To Sleep And Good Nutrition

Children with attention problems need plenty of rest and careful attention to good nutrition. Their behavior usually deteriorates when they are tired or hungry. These children may not be unaware of their own hunger and need to be reminded to eat at regular times. Protein or fruit snacks offered during the middle of the afternoon will help to prevent a disaster around supper time. A good breakfast is especially important for school children.

Getting these children to settle at night can be a difficult job, but unless they get enough sleep, they are irritable and more difficult to manage during the day. A regular bedtime and consistent evening routine are helpful. Children who are very active need time each day to run around and let off energy. Regular exercise will help most children fall sleep more easily.

Some children with attention and mood problems have significant sleep disturbances. Sleep problems must be addressed as part of the child's evaluation.

Educational Planning

Many children with ADD also have learning disabilities. Others do not work up to their academic potential because of problems with attention and distractibility. It is essential for school personnel involved to be aware of the educational needs of each child. Appropriate testing may be needed to clarify a child's strengths and weaknesses.

Children who are not working up to their academic potential should be tested by the school system or a private psychologist. Some of the tests used by schools to identify children who need special educational services are the following:

1. Tests of the child's academic potential. Frequently used tests in this category are the WISC-R, for children 7 and over or the WIPPSI for younger children.
2. Tests of the child's current level of academic achievement. A test used commonly to assess this is the WRAT.

When a learning disability is suspected, additional tests by a specialist in this area may be necessary. Other tests may be needed to identify specific problems in areas such as coordination, balance, motor skills, language and communication.

Therapy

Individual, family and behavior therapy can be an important part of treatment. A therapist may help parents with stressful relationships find better solutions. Parents of difficult children often need support and encouragement. Therapists may also help parents to find their way through the maze of social and judical agencies. Since attention and mood problems are often inherited, it is not uncommon for a parent to realize that he or she might benefit from professional treatment for attention or mood problems. A therapist may be able to help a child develop more appropriate social skills and more positive self-esteem. Children from abusive homes may need long-term therapy in order to form positive relationships with caring adults and to deal with their anger.

Children with ADD are frequently difficult to raise. Even experienced, skilled parents find themselves in "hot water" with these children. Many parents find behavioral management classes or reading material very valuable. This may be in the form of reading (see chapter on Management Techniques), group courses or individual counseling.

Medication

Medication is often an important part of the treatment plan for children with moderate to severe ADD. When children are medicated appropriately, management techniques are more likely to be effective. Many people fear medication, thinking it will change or sedate the child into better behavior or cause permanent harm to the child. The potential benefits and risks of medication must be weighed carefully. The majority of children who are treated with medication for attention and mood problems have no adverse effects from the medicines. All medications have some possibility of causing unwanted side effects or more serious reactions. The side effects from the medications most commonly used to treat attention and mood problems are described in the chapters on medication. Children on any long-term medication must be closely monitored by a knowledgeable physician.

Medications used in the treatment of attention deficit disorders should improve the child's ability to concentrate, stay on task and lessen impulsivity and distractibility. There should be a clearly demonstrable improvement in the child's ability to attend and concentrate with the medication. At the same time, there should be no change in the child's personality or spirit. When medication is effective, teachers are likely to comment that the child is happier, is able to finish assignments, no longer gets into trouble, writes more clearly, and attends to directions better. Children often describe the changes with medication in similar words. When medication is prescribed, the physician should provide information about potential short-term and long-term risks, side effects and necessary follow-up for the parents. If the treatment being suggested is unusual or not customary for ADD, parents should be aware of this and give informed consent prior to the start of treatment. If problems develop, contact your child's physician. Careful monitoring of medication is essential to be sure your child is taking the right medication at the most effective dosage.

There are several "rating scales" that parents and school personnel may use to document behavior changes before and after medication. These rating scales can be customized for each child by picking several target and rating them on a daily basis. School personnel can also observe the child and time the child's "on" and "off" task behavior before and while on medication. This information can be very helpful in deciding if medication is beneficial or if one medication is better than another.

Some doctors recommend a "blind trial" of medication for children with ADD. The child takes medication for one or two weeks, and then takes no medication or a placebo (pill containing no medication but looks just like the medication) for one or two weeks. The parents and teachers rate the child's behavior daily or weekly without knowing if the child is on medication or on placebo. Because of the individual characteristics of the medications used to treat ADD, blind trials may be difficult to do. Cylert and the tricyclics do not lend themselves to this kind of trial because their positive effects may not be seen for 2 to 5 weeks. Blind trials with Ritalin or Dexadrine can be done if several dose levels are included in the trail. Too little Ritalin or Dexadrine will not change the child's behavior and too much will cause the child to be sluggish or irritable. The right dose of medication is different for each child. Medication trials must be done slowly and carefully to give accurate information.

Stimulant medications are the most frequently prescribed for children with ADD. The tricyclics may be used if a child is unable to tolerate stimulants, has had motor tic's, or has a strong family history of affective disorders. Some children show some improvement with stimulants initially but can not tolerate increases in their medication without having significant side-effects. These children may do much better when a tricyclic is added in the evening to the stimulant medication given during the day. Children who become depressed or very angry on stimulants may do better with a tricyclic at night but continue to have problems with attention and distractibility until a stimulant is added again during the day. The combination of the tricyclic and stimulant may be more effective for these children than either one medication alone. Children with very severe affective disorders in addition to their attention problems may benefit from treatment with lithium or a combination of lithium and a tricyclic. Most of these very difficult children have close family members with severe affective disorders. Tegretol is also used to treat manic depressive disorders, particularly when there is a question of a seizure disorder, abnormal EEG or if lithium is poorly tolerated.

Diet And Vitamins

Researchers have been looking at the relationship between diet and hyperactivity for many years. Careful clinical trials have failed to find a significant connection between specific foods, especially those containing sugar, artificial colors or additives, and behavior in the majority of ADD or normal children. Rarely a child's behavior will improve when certain foods are restricted. There is no harm in temporarily eliminating certain foods from a child's diet. Sugar (candy, cookies, cake, sweetened cereals, etc.), artificially flavored and colored foods and medicines (particularly red coloring) are felt by advocates of this theory to be the most common offenders. Long-term changes in a child's diet should be discussed with the child's physician.

Large doses of certain vitamins (Megavitamins) have been promoted as curing various medical problems including ADD symptoms. There is no scientific evidence that this treatment is effective. Large doses of certain vitamins can cause serious problems. If you have questions about unusual treatments or "cures" for ADD consult your child's physician.

5

Learning Disabilities

What Is A Learning Disability?

The term "learning disability" (LD) refers to problems that adults or children may have with learning and processing information. A person with a learning disability may have difficulty listening, speaking, remembering, reading, writing, reasoning or problem-solving. The learning disability creates a discrepancy between the child's potential ability and actual performance. Learning problems range from mild to very severe. Even though some children with learning disabilities have other handicapping conditions (e.g., problems with vision, hearing, mental retardation, social and emotional disturbances), the learning disability is not the direct result of these conditions. Learning disabilities may occur together with other environmental influences (e.g., cultural differences, insufficient or inappropriate instruction, psychological factors), but are not the direct result of these influences. (Adapted from definition in an article by Meyers and Hammill, Bulletin of the Orton Society, 1982). Many professionals include problems with attention, concentration and distractibility within their definition of learning disabilities. Learning disabilities are seen in children who are superior, above average, average or below average in intelligence. LD children often have excellent abilities in many areas of learning (e.g. understanding complicated concepts, musical abilities, long-term memory) and severe difficulties in other areas (e.g. expressing thoughts clearly, short-term memory, sequencing, reading comprehension). It is hard to generalize about children with learning disabilities because each child's strengths and weaknesses are unique.

Some professionals in this field who believe that children have learning differences, rather than disorders, feel the real problem lies within our educational system. Some children need information presented in a way that is different for them to make use of it. Teachers with twenty or more students don't have the time and frequently don't have the training to figure out how each of these children learn most effectively.

What Is The Difference Between Learning Disabilities And Mental Retardation?

Mental retardation is a term that describes a severe impairment in almost all areas of the child's functioning including learning ability, gross and fine motor maturation and social adjustment. The handicaps in learning and understanding are especially severe.

Children with learning disabilities may have good to superior learning and thinking abilities in many areas, despite difficulties in one or more areas.

How Do Schools Define Learning Disabilities?

The Department of Public Instruction in each state is responsible for setting that state's "working" definition of the term "learning disability." It is necessary for each school system to have uniform criteria for children who will receive special educational instruction. Currently, the Wisconsin definition for entry into a learning disability class consists of two parts:

1. The child must exhibit normal or the potential for normal intellectual functioning based on information obtained using standard intelligence testing.
2. The child must be performing at or below 50% of the expected level of achievement in two or more areas of the readiness or basic skill areas of math, reading, spelling and written language.

This means that a second grade student might qualify if he or she was tested at or below first grade level in at least two areas. A student in tenth grade must be at or below the fifth grade level in order to qualify for LD placement in Wisconsin. Obviously, an older student must be having very significant problems in order to receive help. A very bright child with a significant learning problem may never fall far enough behind academically to qualify for help. The criteria for entry into a learning disability program in states other than Wisconsin may differ. Information about the specific guidelines can be obtained from your local school district administration office.

What Kinds Of Problems Do Learning Disabled Children Have?

The following chart (see page 30) is a very simplified diagram of the interrelationships in the processes involved in learning.

Learning disabled children may also develop any of the following problems as a result of living with a chronic disability:

POOR SELF-ESTEEM—Children with learning problems may feel different from their classmates. They may describe themselves as "inferior" or "stupid."

ANTICIPATION OF SCHOOL FAILURE—Based on past school failure, LD children anticipate chronic struggle and failure. Eventually, they may lose interest and stop trying.

INPUT:

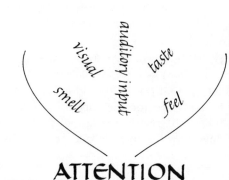

smell *visual* *auditory input* *taste* *feel*

ATTENTION

⬇

CONCENTRATION

**STORAGE ~
INTEGRATION:**

*short term
memory*

*long term
memory*

*integration
sequencing
abstraction
coordination*

RETRIEVAL

OUTPUT:

movement:
- *fine motor*
- *gross motor*
- *balance
  coordination*

*language
communication:*
- *written*
- *oral*

SOCIAL IMMATURITY—Some children with learning disabilities may be immature socially and prefer to play with younger children. The impulsive and inappropriate behavior of other children is a significant problem.

Do All Children With Learning Disabilities Have Trouble In School?

Many children with mild to moderate learning problems do well in school. The difficulty a child has will depend on many things. One is the severity of the learning disorder. Another is the addition of other complicating problems and stresses for the child (e.g. medical illnesses, abuse, family stress, frequent school changes, etc.). For example, a child with a severe learning disorder may be having as much trouble functioning as another child with a mild learning problem who has been abused by a parent and then placed in several foster homes. Children with very severe learning disabilities will be greatly helped by supportive parents who provide educational challenges and enrichment at home.

What Causes Children To Have Learning Disabilities?

It is not always clear what has caused an individual child to have learning problems. Some general causes of learning disabilities have been identified. They include:

GENETIC—Learning disabilities appear to be inherited in certain families. ADD may be present in some family members and learning problems in others. Boys are affected more often than girls.

BRAIN DAMAGE—Brain damage from insults such as infection, injury, exposure to toxic substances can cause learning problems.

MATURATIONAL DELAY—Some children appear to mature more slowly in certain areas. These children do eventually get to a level that is average or above for their age but the process takes longer for them.

NEUROTRANSMITTER DISORDERS—Some researchers feel that learning disabilities (at least in some cases) are caused by an imbalance of the chemicals that send messages between nerve cells within the brain. This is a relatively new area of research and there is much to learn.

How Are Learning Disabilities Diagnosed?

Children can be assessed for learning disabilities by a trained psychologist (either a master's level or Ph.D. with an educational background) or by a learning disabilities specialist. An LD specialist is usually a teacher who has been specially trained to work with and evaluate children with learning problems. Schools may use both psychologists and LD specialists when they evaluate a child for special placement along with other specialists when needed.

How Are Learning Disabilities Treated?

EDUCATIONAL ASSESSMENT—First and foremost, it is essential to know what a child's learning strengths and weaknesses are and how a child learns best. All other problems (medical, psychological and social) should be clearly defined before a treatment plan is formulated.

EDUCATIONAL TREATMENT PLAN—The school personnel or psychologist who has evaluated the child should provide an individual educational plan for the child. This may include any combination of the following: placement in a special class, help from a tutor or private educational specialist, speech and language help, physical or occupational therapy, suggestions for educational materials and techniques that are appropriate for the child's problems, counseling, etc. Some of these services will be provided by the school and others must be arranged and paid for by the family. Special private schools for children with learning disabilities may be appropriate. Some universities have programs designed to help their learning disabled students.

ADVOCACY—Children with learning disabilities need strong advocates who will continually reassess the child's needs and find resources for the child and family. It is important for parents to be knowledgeable about the educational rights of their children. Many states have parent organizations or legal advocacy groups that provide this information.

MEDICAL EVALUATION—A careful and thorough examination should identify other medical problems. It may be necessary to seek specialized help to identify children who have ADD symptoms as a part of their learning problems.

MEDICAL INTERVENTION—Since many children have ADD as a part of their learning disability, medical treatment for ADD should be considered when appropriate. Other medical problems must also be treated appropriately.

BUILDING POSITIVE SELF-ESTEEM—Parents and educators who work with children with learning problems must continually work at building positive self-esteem in these children and other children with handicaps. Humiliation of a child or unfair criticism of the child's work is never an appropriate educational or parenting technique.

COUNSELING AND THERAPY—It may be important to seek the help of a counselor, psychologist or psychiatrist if the child is having significant problems with self-esteem, depression, social maturity or if the family is under undue stress.

SUGGESTED READINGS ABOUT LEARNING DISABILITIES

Silver, Larry. *The Misunderstood Child; A Handbook For Parents With Children with Learning Disabilities.* New York: McGraw Hill. 1985. Hardcover. 200 pages. About $15.00. This clear, informative book for parents and educators is about the diagnosis, evaluation, and treatment of children with Learning Disabilities. Attention Deficit Disorders are considered by the author to be one of many different learning problems children may have. Dr. Silver is a well-known expert in this field and his clear writing makes a very confusing, difficult subject understandable.

Smith, Sally L. *No Easy Answers, The Learning Disabled Child At Home And At School.* Bantum books, 1978, paperback, about $4.00, 270 pages. This book is almost entirely about children with learning disabilities and helping parents understand their special educational needs. Included is a lengthy discussion about the legal obligations of the school to provide individual educational programs for these children. There is an extensive annotated bibliography and information about support groups and resources.

Clark, Louise. *Can't Read, Can't Write, Can't Talk Too Good Either.* Walker and Co., 1973, 270 pages. The first half of this book describes Mrs. Clark's son's struggles with dyslexia. When he entered school in the 1950's, very little information was available about this problem. In spite of severe academic problems, this very bright youngster managed to struggle through college and then graduate school. His battles, and those of his parents, are poignantly described. In the second half of the book Mrs. Clark describes returning to the schools that worked with her son twenty years earlier. She examines their current programs for children with dyslexia.

Bryan, Tanis & James H. Bryan. *Understanding Learning Disabilities.* Palo Alto, Cal.:Mayfield Publishing, 1986. Third edition. 442 pages. This is a useful and complete textbook for students in the field of education.

6

Affective Disorders

What Are Affective Disorders And What Causes Them?

Affective disorders are a group of dis-orders (something is out of order or out of balance in the body) that cause a change in how a person feels and functions. Mood (sadness, irritability, reactivity, guilt, anxiety) and daily routine (sleep, appetite, energy level) are affected. Affective disorders are caused by imbalances in chemicals that send messages from one nerve cell to another within the nervous system. These chemicals are called neuro-transmitters. There are many different neurotransmitters within the brain. Because these neurotransmitters are present in very, very small amounts in the brain, it has been hard to develop specific tests for these disorders. The tests available at this time are expensive, and not always accurate. There is very little information about the use of this kind of testing in children.

Other names are occasionally used to refer to "affective disorders." The most common are "endogenous depressive disorder", "unipolar depressive disorder", "dysthymic disorder" and "mood disorder." Manic depressive disorder (also called "bipolar affective disorder") is a less common and usually more severe form of affective disorder.

How Does Someone Get An Affective Disorder?

Affective disorders are not contagious. A vulnerability for mood disorders is thought to be inherited or passed on from one generation to another in the same way that a predisposition for other physical illnesses is inherited (asthma, high blood pressure, and bleeding problems, for example). Exactly how this vulnerability is inherited is not well understood. It is often possible to trace back and find other family members with similar mood problems. Current research indicates that as many as one in every ten people may have a problem with an affective disorder at some time during their life.

Mood disorders, like other physical ailments, may be acute (where there is a sudden change in mood or affect lasting at least two weeks) or chronic (where long standing problems are present with minor fluctuations for months or years). Affective disorders may be made worse by illness (i.e. ear infections), hormone changes (i.e. puberty or following childbirth), or stress (the death of a parent, a difficult divorce). At other times, it is impossible to find a cause that has precipitated the change in mood.

What Are The Symptoms Of Affective Disorders?

Like other medical illnesses, there are many different ways a person may show symptoms of these disorders. The symptoms in adults are better defined than in children. In adults, the underlying complaint is usually unpleasant mood or depression. Most people experience loss of interest or pleasure in many of their daily activities. These symptoms tend to persist for weeks or longer. Other symptoms that are common in adults include:

1. Loss of appetite or increase in eating
2. Trouble with sleep, waking early in the morning and not being able to get back to sleep or trouble getting to sleep at night
3. Restlessness, pacing, hand-wringing, inability to sit still
4. Slowed speech, or slowed activity and dullness
5. Feeling tired in the absence of physical activity
6. Feeling of worthlessness or guilt
7. Difficulty concentrating, making decisions or thinking
8. Thoughts of death or suicide or suicidal attempts
9. Tearfulness, feelings of anxiety, irritability, fear, brooding, excessive worry about physical health or appearance, or panic attacks

The listing above is adapted from *Diagnostic and Statistical Manual of Mental Disorders* (Third Edition), page 223. (Used with permission of the American Psychiatric Association.)

Children and adolescents may have any of the symptoms described above or may be irritable, afraid to leave their parents, or very moody with extremes of anger or sadness. School performance may drop because of poor interest, restlessness or poor concentration. Some adolescents lose weight, vomit after meals or binge on certain foods while others have increased appetite. Other children become very frightened or may have periods of being extremely anxious. Headaches, abdominal pain, compulsive behavior, unusual concern about cleanliness or body functioning may also be seen. Some children will refuse to go to school and become "school phobic." Rarely a child will set fires, think about or attempt suicide. Some children have stool soiling and night time wetting (enuresis). Each child presents a different picture and sorting out the exact problem may take time and the input of various health professionals.

What Is The Difference Between
Unipolar And Bipolar Affective Disorder?

Unipolar affective disorder is the most common form of affective disorder. Bipolar disorders are less common and often more severe. People with bipolar disorders (manic depressive illness) initially have the same symptoms described above for affective disorders. They develop mood swings, explosive rage or recurrent changes in mood in later years. The manic phase of this illness can last hours or weeks. Symptoms of mania may include significant irritability, restlessness, activity that appears to be driven or pressured, continuous talking, inappropriately happy or euphoric mood, grandiose thoughts, poor judgment, behavior that mimics intoxication without the benefit of drugs or alcohol, inability to sleep and/or delusions.

How Are Affective Disorders Diagnosed?

Affective disorders are most often diagnosed after detailed information is obtained about current problems, home and school behavior (past and present), past medical history, family history and a physical examination. A physician (M.D.), psychiatrist (M.D.–with psychiatric training), psychologist (M.S. or Ph.D.), or social worker (M.S.W.) may be trained to diagnose these disorders. Information obtained from a child's school is also helpful. Laboratory tests to rule out other physical disorders that can cause similar symptoms may be indicated. Psychological testing may also give important information. A careful and thorough evaluation may take several hours and the input of more than one health professional.

How Are Children With Affective Disorders Treated?

Children with affective disorders and their families frequently struggle for years before the disorder is recognized.

Recommendations for treatment must be individualized for each child. The professional evaluating your child should help you understand how the diagnosis was formulated and what particular pieces of information were important in drawing those conclusions. Treatment choices (pro's and con's of each) should be fully discussed before treatment is started. The following are important parts of the treatment plan.

MEDICATION—The tricyclic medications are used most often in the medical treatment of mood disorders in children. In special situations, lithium, carbamazepine (Tegretol) and some of the newer medications that are used in the treatment of adults with mood disorders may be necessary.

THERAPY—Both the family and the child with a mood disorder may benefit from some form of therapy. Children with mood disorders have an altered view of their world and of themselves. A therapist can help them to see their true selves more clearly and to understand where the disorder has taken away their control and distorted their perceptions.

Children with mood disorders are usually a challenge for even the most patient and skilled parents. Therapy can help to support parents through difficult problems and also provide fresh insights and ideas for management.

Young children can not be expected to sit in the therapist's office and talk for any length of time about themselves. Therapy with young children is usually done within the context of a play activity. Children are more comfortable dealing with their problems in an indirect way. For example, a young child may be able to express anger using puppets or dolls, but may not be able to talk about it directly.

EDUCATION—The family and professionals that interact with the child must understand what the problem is and in what ways it is being treated. The child should be given age-appropriate information so that she can be an active participant in the treatment.

> *Molly, who is five years old, is about to be started on a tricyclic at bedtime to treat her mood disorder. The doctor tells her, "Molly, you know that I've been talking with you and your mother and father about how we can make things better at home. I know you don't like being so frightened at night, and I don't think you like feeling so sad. I am going to give your parents a prescription for medicine to help make those sad and scary feelings go away. When you come back to see me next time, I'd like you to tell me how you are feeling."*

SUPPORT—Parents of difficult children can find comfort and share important resources with each other. Many parts of the country have support groups for parents of learning disabled, difficult, hyperactive, or emotionally disturbed children. (See chapter on resources).

Who Should Treat The Child With An Affective Disorder?

Medical treatment for affective disorders must be prescribed by an M.D., usually a psychiatrist who works with children. Not all medical doctors are knowledgeable about these disorders or their treatment. When educational and psychological testing are needed, this should be done by a psychologist (either a master's level professional or a Ph.D.). Other psychologists as well as some social workers and psychiatrists are trained as therapists offering individual and family therapy and counseling. Behavioral management programs and counseling may be offered by psychiatrists, psychologists, social workers or pediatricians.

SUGGESTED READINGS ON AFFECTIVE DISORDERS

GENERAL INFORMATION

Greist, John and J. Jefferson. *Depression And Its Treatment.* Washington, D.C.: American Psychiatric Press. 112 Pages, Paperback, $7.95. This is an excellent book that explains in simple language the causes and current treatment for depressive or affective disorders.

Wender, Paul and D. Klein. *Mind, Mood And Medicine.* New York: Meridian. paperback, 372 pages, about $ 8.00. This excellent book provides easily understood information about diagnosis and treatment of affective disorders, schizophrenia, anxiety disorders, obsessive-compulsive disorders, and other mental health problems. Actual case histories help to make this a very interesting and readable book.

AFFECTIVE DISORDERS IN CHILDREN

Weller, Elizabeth and R. Weller, Editors. *Major Depressive Disorders In Children, Clinical Insights Monograph Series.* American Psychiatric Press, Inc. 95 pages. Paperback. Short but excellent book about depression in children. Includes historical and theoretical perspectives, assessment and treatment, familial aspects, use of tricyclic antidepressants in the young child with depression, and an overview of the status of childhood depression.

Cantwell, Dennis and G. Carlson, Editors. *Affective Disorders In Childhood And Adolescence, An Update.* New York: Spectrum Publications. 1983. 475 Pages. Hard cover. $35.00. Excellent major textbook about affective disorders in children. Included are comprehensive chapters on medication and behavioral therapy.

7

Evaluating the Child with Attention, Learning and Behavioral Problems

A thorough and comprehensive evaluation is the only way to identify the many factors that contribute to a child's attention, behavior and learning problems. Information should be obtained from as many participants in the child's environment as possible (current and past schools, baby sitter, current and past physicians, previous hospital admission summaries, social service agencies, therapists).

The initial focus of the evaluation is to describe the learning and behavior problems as seen by the child, family and school. In order to assess the "whole picture", the evaluator must gather additional information so that each child's unique situation is completely understood. Frequently, past or present unrecognized problems are identified that affect the diagnosis and treatment plan.

What Are Some Of The More Common Problems That Affect Children's Learning And Behavior?

MEDICAL—Recurrent ear infections especially in the first three years of life, long-standing mild to moderate hearing loss, poor vision, growth retardation, inadequate nutrition, incomplete bladder or bowel control during the day or night, constipation, incomplete immunizations, anemia, thyroid gland abnormalities, pin worms, allergies, asthma.

NEUROLOGIC—Migraine, seizure disorders, ticcing disorders, degenerative neurologic disorders.

INHERITED—Tuberous sclerosis, neurofibromatosis, fragile X syndrome.

ENVIRONMENTAL—Lead poisoning.

EDUCATIONAL—Unrecognized learning problems, inappropriate school placement, inappropriate educational expectations.

PAST MEDICAL INSULTS—Spinal meningitis, severe head injury, fetal alcohol syndrome.

SOCIAL—Family stress from divorce, abuse, neglect, mental health problems in a parent, inadequate parental management skills.

What Information Should Be Included In A Comprehensive Assessment?

Since a complete assessment involves a large volume of information, it must be organized in a manageable form. The following illustrates how this might be done. Structure and organization helps ensure thoroughness. The style and orientation of the evaluator will influence how this information is obtained and organized.

CHIEF COMPLAINT—Description of the child's current problems at home and at school.

HISTORY OF PRESENTING PROBLEMS—History of the evolution of each of these problems. When were they first noticed? How did they evolve? What has influenced them? Are they constant? How do they vary? What has been done in the past that has or has not been useful?

PHYSICAL ASSESSMENT—Child's current physical health assessed by a recent complete physical exam (including a careful neurologic assessment). This is usually done by a physician specializing in pediatrics or pediatric neurology. Hearing and vision assessment by an optometrist or ophthalmologist are important for all children with learning or behavioral problems.

PAST MEDICAL HISTORY—Descriptions of the child's past medical problems, operations, hospitalizations, accidents, injuries, seizures, allergies, hearing problems.

BIRTH HISTORY—Prenatal, birth and postnatal history, exposure to drugs and alcohol, prematurity, need for resuscitation at birth, problems during pregnancy, labor, delivery or shortly afterwards.

DAILY HABITS—Information about sleeping, eating, bowel and bladder habits, toilet training, diet and daily routine.

DEVELOPMENTAL HISTORY—When did the child acquire developmental milestones (rolling over, sitting, walking, first words, sentences)? How are the child's fine and gross motor skills, balance, speech, language and communication development?

TEMPERAMENT—Have there been problems with aggression, anxieties, compulsive behaviors, adaptability, ritualistic or compulsive behavior, activity level, distractibility, impulsivity, organizational skills, mood, or temper tantrums. What discipline techniques have been tried?

SCHOOL HISTORY—What is the current placement? Does the child get any special help? Has the child repeated grades? Information should be obtained from the current teacher about concerns, strengths and problems. Past school testing, evaluations and old report cards should be reviewed.

SOCIAL HISTORY—Information should be obtained bout the child's family and daily life experiences, marrital problems, recent loss or change in the household, divorce, abuse, neglect, foster care, involvement with other social service agencies or problems with the law.

FAMILY HISTORY—Behavior and learning problems, hyperactivity, learning problems, psychiatric problems and hospitalizations, seizure disorders, depression, anxiety, suicide, drug and alcohol abuse, unexplained death, retardation.

PAST TREATMENT—Reports from other agencies, physicians and therapists, unsuccessful and successful interventions by the school and family.

CLINICAL OBSERVATIONS—Observations of the child and the family in the office and on occasion, in school or at home.

ADDITIONAL INFORMATION—Assessments may be needed from specialists in such areas as learning disabilities, psychology, psychiatry, neurology, neuropsychology, speech and language, physical or occupational therapy.

After the problems are identified, the treatment plan can be formulated. The clinician evaluating the child should offer to review the problem list and the treatment plan with the parents. Parents are entitled to this information and may request it specifically if it is not offered. Ask for clarification in non-technical language. Treatment should be undertaken only after a working diagnosis is formulated and discussed with the child's parents.

What Other Information Should The Evaluation Provide?

Parents should have the opportunity to discuss the pro's and con's of various treatment options with the professionals who evaluate their child.

This discussion may include information about hazards, side effects, anticipated positive effects, length of anticipated treatment, length of time until change is seen and the possibilities of "no benefit" from each treatment option. Parents should ask about the frequency of follow-up appointments and tests, including blood levels for specific medication.

What To Look For When Choosing A Health Professional.

The ideal professional to evaluate your child should be experienced in evaluating and treating children with learning or behavioral problems. The professional should be responsible, compassionate, available when needed for office appointments and phone consultations, and willing to communicate regularly with the child, the parents and the child's school. This professional should be willing to work as part of a team that includes the child, the child's parents and siblings, the child's teachers and other health professionals. The goal of this team should be to enable the child and his or her family to function at the highest level possible. This professional respects the information and expertise of the other members of the team (including the child and the child's parents). This professional seeks to share his or her information with the child and family because she or he believes that the more knowledgeable the child and family are, the more helpful they will be as part of the treatment team. The professional values the information and questions parents bring and openly discusses their concerns with them. This professional refers the child and family to other community resources when appropriate and informs the family when she or he is in need of consultation with other experts when concerns go beyond his or her knowledge or area of expertise.

What Kind Of Professional Should Evaluate
A Child With Behavioral And Learning Problems?

Ideally, the evaluation (intake) should be done by a SKILLED and UNBIASED professional (or a team of professionals) who is able to provide a comprehensive multisystem evaluation, formulate a treatment plan, discuss treatment choices and options with the family and child when appropriate, and then refer the family to other professionals or services with the intent of making the best match for the child and family's unique needs. This person might be a pediatric neurologist, a behavioral or developmental pediatrician, a child psychiatrist or a child psychologist. If a physician (M.D.) does the initial evaluation, he or she may need to have a psychologist review testing materials or a social worker gather information about the family. If a psychologist or social worker evaluates the child, a physician should obtain the medical information (including a thorough physical exam). Some families will decide after completion of the evaluation to have the same professional treat their child or coordinate the treatment plan that has been formulated.

Suggestions For Finding Skilled Professionals.

Try to gather information from many different sources. The following are suggestions for starting the search. Call or write the local chapter of the Association for Children with Learning Disabilities. Look in the phone book for social service agencies that work with children. Ask which specialists they use when they refer a child for learning and behavioral problems. Ask your child's teacher, the school psychologist, school social worker, nurse or principal for the names of professionals they like to work with. If there is a medical school or university in the area, ask for information from any of the following departments: Pediatrics, Psychiatry, Psychology, Educational Psychology, Child and Family Studies, School of Education. Talk to friends or people at work. Information from people who work in the medical or educational fields can be particularly helpful.

What Information Should A Parent Request When Scheduling The Evaluation?

It is reasonable to ask how long the evaluation will take, who will see the child, what kind of testing will be done, how much the evaluation will cost and how much your insurance will pay.

The evaluation process can be very stressful and intimidating. Some people find it helpful to bring a friend, family member or person from the child's school along for the evaluation. It is difficult for a parent to remember all of the information that is presented. Ask if the evaluation can be taped so that the information can be reviewed later or shared with other family members and school personnel. Write down a list of questions that you want to discuss before you go to an appointment.

How Severe Should A Child's Problem Be Before Treatment Is Started?

There are no clear rules or guidelines. The decision is an individual one and will vary somewhat from one professional to another. Clinicians have different orientations "for" or "against" various kinds of treatment based on their training or background and this will also influence their decision. Treatment is usually considered when a child's problems are interfering significantly with learning and behavior at home and/or at school. The decision to start medical treatment will be very clear for most children. These children have severe problems at home and at school. They may be in special classrooms in school and may not be able to keep up with the academic work. Their parents may have significant trouble at home with behavior and management. For other children the problems are less severe. Ultimately, the decision of when to treat and what treatment to undertake must be made by the child's parents with the support and guidance of their health professionals.

Why Do Professionals Disagree About
A Child's Specific Diagnosis?

For some children, there may be disagreement about the child's diagnosis. The question of "what is being treated" can be a controversial one. There are no laboratory tests to help us clarify diagnosis for children with learning and behavioral problems. There are guidelines such as the *Diagnostic and Statistical Manual* used by many professionals but within them, there is much left for interpretation. The training and orientation of the professional may also affect how a problem is seen and also treated. Two professionals trained in two very different schools may see the same child and differ significantly in their diagnostic and treatment formulations.

8

Information About Stimulant Medications

PEMOLINE (Cylert)

What Is Pemoline Used For And How Does It Work?

Pemoline (trade name is Cylert) is a medication that is used to treat hyperactivity and attention deficit disorders in children and adults. This is its only medical use. Pemoline increases attention span and concentration, lessens distractibility and impulsiveness in children with attention deficits. In some children there is improvement in perceptual motor skills (handwriting becomes neater). Children who are hyperactive seem more focused and are better able to handle unstructured situations. Pemoline is not a tranquilizer and is not addictive.

How Is Pemoline Given?

Pemoline is given orally to the child every morning with breakfast. It's duration of action is about 18 to 24 hours. In some children the benefits from the medication are not seen until the medication has been taken for 2 to 4 weeks. In other children improvement is seen within the first week. Pemoline tablets come in two strengths, 37.5 mg. and 75 mg. The 37.5 mg. tablet is available in an orange flavored chewable tablet. The chewable tablets are more expensive. All of the tablets are scored and can be cut in half with a sharp knife.

Children who have difficulty only in school should start pemoline a few weeks before they return in the fall and continue the medication until school is over in the spring. Pemoline should be given on weekends and during school vacations in order to ensure optimal benefit from the medication. Children who have significant problems at home and at school may continue to take pemoline during the summer months as well. All children should stop pemoline for a brief period each year to reevaluate the effectiveness of this medication.

It is important to start and stop pemoline gradually. Children often become irritable and complain of headaches when this medicine is stopped suddenly.

What Side Effects Does Pemoline Have?

Like all medications, pemoline occasionally causes side effects. For most children, these side effects are minimal. Any problems that may be due to medication should be reported to the child's physician.

Pemoline may cause stomach aches especially when the child takes the medication on an empty stomach. Usually this can be avoided by taking the medication with breakfast. Some children have trouble falling asleep for the first few days on this medication or for a few days after the dose is increased. Increasing the dose in smaller steps helps to lessen this. Occasionally a child will continue to have significant problems getting to sleep. Pemoline should be discontinued if the sleep problems are severe or show no improvement within a short time. Children occasionally become irritable when the dose is increased. This irritability is usually temporary. Irritability may also mean that the dose of pemoline is too high for the particular child. Headaches may be a problem in some children while on pemoline. If they are severe or frequent, the child's physician should be notified.

Pemoline may suppress a child's appetite during the first few weeks of treatment. Children should be weighed and followed regularly by their physician. The weight loss is rarely more than two or three pounds. Most children regain the lost weight after the first month of treatment.

Research studies in the past suggested that Pemoline lessened the rate of growth of children who took this medication all year long. More recent studies indicate that children on pemoline grow regularly after the first year. If there is a slight slowing of the growth rate at all, there appears to be a "catch-up" growth spurt during the following year. Children on pemoline should have their height and weight checked at regular intervals by their physician.

Very unusual reactions to pemoline include skin rash or unusual movements of the tongue and face. Rarely a child will develop a change in liver function. Regular blood tests to check the child's liver function are recommended. These side effects are very uncommon and should go away when the medicine is stopped.

Children who have epilepsy or abnormal EEG tests (electroencephalograms) should be started on pemoline very carefully. Stimulant medications lower the seizure threshold of the brain. A child with seizures will be more likely to have a seizure when taking this medication. Careful monitoring of stimulant medication and medications for the control of seizures are very important in children with seizure disorders. Rarely, a child will have a first seizure while on stimulant medication. These children have had previously unrecognized seizure disorders. Treatment of the underlying seizure disorder must be undertaken first and then treatment for ADD can be attempted carefully.

Are There Any Reasons Why A Child Should Not Take Pemoline?

Children with a history or family history of motor tics or Tourette's syndrome (abnormal and uncontrollable movements of certain muscle groups) often have significant problems with ADD. When these children are treated with stimulant medication, their ticcing disorder may get worse. Other medications such as the tricyclics, should be used to treat these children for their attention problems when possible. If stimulant medication is recommended for these children, a physician who is very experienced in using these medications should monitor the child closely.

Are there any medications a child should not take while on Pemoline?
Pemoline can be given safely with other medications. However, the physician who is treating a child's attention problems should be aware of any other medications your child uses regularly.

METHYLPHENIDATE (Ritalin) and DEXTROAMPHETAMINE (Dexedrine)

What Are Methylphenidate And Dextroamphetamine Used For And How Do They Work?
Methylphenidate (trade name is Ritalin) and Dextroamphetamine (trade name is Dexedrine) are medications used to treat attention deficit disorders in children and adults, narcolepsy (a sleep disorder of adults) and treatment-resistant depression in adults. Their affects on the nervous system are similar to norepinephrine, a naturally occurring chemical (neurotransmitter) found in the brain. Like pemoline, methylphenidate and dextroamphetamine lessen distractibility, improve concentration and in some children improve perceptual-motor abilities. Hyperactive children are better able to organize their actions and are less impulsive.

How is Methylphenidate given?
Methylphenidate comes in pill form and is taken by mouth. It is available in three strengths, 5 mg., 10 mg., 20 mg. The duration of action of methylphenidate is three to four hours. Most children take methylphenidate two or three times each day. It is usually given with breakfast and at lunchtime. A third dose may be needed early in the afternoon. A longer acting formulation of methylphenidate (Ritalin 20SR) is also available. It has a duration of action of six to eight hours. The Ritalin 20 SR is actually equivalent to the dose of 10 mg. regular methylphenidate but with a longer duration of action. For some children, Ritalin 20 SR eliminates the need to give a dose of medication at lunchtime.

How Is Dextroamphetamine Given?
Dextroamphetamine is given by mouth and is available as an elixir, tablet and long-acting spansule. The elixir and tablet have a duration of

action of about four to six hours. The spansule is usually effective for eight to twelve hours. The elixir is orange flavored and comes in one strength (5 mg. per teaspoon). The tablets are scored and come in only the 5mg. strength. The spansule comes in 5mg., 10 mg. and 15 mg. strengths.

How Long Does It Take To See A Change In Behavior With These Medications?

Unlike pemoline, the effect of methylphenidate and dextroamphetamine may be seen within the first day of its use. Most children take methylphenidate and dextroamphetamine daily. If a child is only having problems at school, the medication can be given on school days and omitted during weekends and vacations. If a child is having significant problems at home and at school, this medication can be given daily during entire year. As with pemoline, children should be taken off stimulant medication for a brief period each year to be sure the medication is effective.

In high doses, both methylphenidate and dextroamphetamine have the potential for abuse and addiction. Addiction occurs in adults and teens who regularly abuse very high doses. Researchers have followed children with attention problems who have taken methylphenidate and dextroamphetamine into their teens and adult years. They found that these children are no more likely than any other group of teens to abuse other drugs. Changes in the dose of methylphenidate and dextroamphetamine may be necessary as children gain weight and grow.

What Side Effects Do Methylphenidate and Dextroamphetamine Have?

Some children have a decrease in appetite while on methylphenidate and dextroamphetamine. In these children, the medication is best given after breakfast and after lunch. Some children have mild changes in heart rate and blood pressure. Children on stimulant medication should have regular physical examination including measurements of height, weight and blood pressure. Rarely, there will be a change in a child's blood count with the medication and a blood test may be necessary if the child seems unusually prone to infection. Occasionally a child will complain of headaches. If the headaches become severe or continue to occur, the medication may have to be discontinued.

Like pemoline, methylphenidate and dextroamphetamine may cause minimal lessening of the growth rate during the first year the medication is prescribed. Recent studies indicate that children on methylphenidate and dextroamphetamine for periods longer than one year resume normal growth rates and grow to expected adult heights. This new information is reassuring. Weight and height checks continue to be an important part of follow-up care for any child on these medications. Children who are very small (at or below the 3rd percentile in height) because of other medical problems should be followed more carefully to be sure their growth continues at an acceptable rate.

Children who have epilepsy or abnormal EEG tests (electroencephalograms) should be started on these medications very carefully. Stimulant medications lower the seizure threshold of the brain. A child with a tendency to have seizures will be more likely to have a seizure when taking this medication. Careful monitoring of the stimulant medication and medications for the control of seizures are very important in these children. Rarely, a child will have a first seizure while on stimulant medication. These children usually have abnormal EEG's, but have never been diagnosed as having a seizure disorder prior to the start of this medication. Treatment of the underlying seizure disorder must be undertaken first and then treatment for ADD can be attempted carefully.

Are There Any Reasons Why A Child Should Not Take Methylphenidate or Dextroamphetamine?

Methylphenidate and dextroamphetamine are both broken down in the body by the liver. Children on antidepressants and seizure medications need to have the doses of these medications monitored carefully if stimulants are prescribed.

Children who have a history of motor tics, Tourette's syndrome or who have a family member with a ticcing disorder frequently have ADD symptoms. Stimulant medication may make motor ticcing worse. These children should be treated initially with other medications. If it is necessary to give methylphenidate or dextroamphetamine, these children must be monitored very closely by physicians who are experienced in the use of these medications.

What Is The Difference Between Methylphenidate And Dextroamphetamine?

Methylphenidate and dextroamphetamine are both amphetamines. Their chemical composition is very similar. Dextroamphetamine is thought to have slightly more potential for abuse in very high doses, much higher than those used to treat ADD children. Dextroamphetamine is less expensive and is available in several formulations. The long-acting spansule is also available in several strengths. The duration of action of the regular dextroamphetamine tablets is longer than that of regular methylphenidate tablets.

If A Child Does Not Respond Well To One Of The Stimulants, Will The Response Be Better If Another Stimulant Is Used?

Children respond differently to each of the stimulants. A child may do beautifully with dextroamphetamine and have problems with methylphenidate, or beautifully with pemoline and be intolerant of Ritalin. It is very difficult to predict how a child will respond to each of these medications.

9

Information About Tricyclics

The tricyclics are a family of medicines with very similar chemical structures. They are used to treat children and adults with ADD, sleep disorders, anxiety disorders, bedwetting and biologic depression (affective disorder). The tricyclics most frequently prescribed for children are listed below with their generic and trade names (in parenthesis):

Imipramine (Tofranil)—10 mg., 25 mg., 50 mg.,
small coated tablets

Nortriptyline (Pamelor)—10 mg., 25 mg., 50 mg., 75 mg.
(Aventil) capsules and liquid (10 mg./5cc)

Amitriptyline (Elavil)—10 mg., 25 mg., 50 mg., 100 mg.,
150 mg., small coated tablet

Desipramine (Norpramin)—25 mg., 50 mg., 75 mg., 100 mg.,
(Pertofrane) 150 mg., small coated tablets

How Do The Tricyclics Work?

These medicines correct an imbalance in the chemicals (called neurotransmitters) within the nervous system that cause biologic depressive illness (affective disorder). When the neurotransmitter imbalance is corrected, mood or affect (energy level, self-esteem, anxiety, depression, irritability, etc.) returns to normal. These medicines have no mood-changing effect in people who do not have biologic depression. These medicines are not "uppers" or "downers" and are not habit-forming or addictive.

Some children with attention deficit disorders show significant improvement when they are treated with tricyclics. Other ADD children show no response to this group of medication. Children with attention problems secondary to an affective disorder are more likely to respond well to the tricyclics. Tricyclics should be considered in ADD children when there is a strong family history of mood disorder, especially if stimulant medication is not tolerated.

How Are Tricyclics Given?

Tricyclics are usually taken by mouth once a day between dinner and bed time. Recent studies indicate that some children metabolize or clear the tricyclics much faster from their bodies than adults do. These children need to take this medication twice a day. The tricyclics must be taken regularly for one to five weeks before improvement is seen in attention or mood. In order to minimize problems with side effects, the dose of the tricyclics is gradually increased over a period of about a week. Because each child metabolizes these medications at different rates, a blood test may be needed to tell if the amount of medicine being taken is enough, too much, or too little.

What Side Effects Do The Tricyclics Cause?

Like all medications, there are occasionally some side effects. These side effects are more likely to be an annoyance than a real problem. Children seem to have less trouble with side effects than adults do when taking tricyclics. If a child has a problem with one of the side effects, contact your physician. It may be necessary to change to a different tricyclic, give the medication at a different time, or to alter the dose.

The most common side effects are dry mouth, sleepiness and constipation. Special care should be taken with cleaning the teeth since dryness of the mouth is due to a decrease in the production of saliva and saliva helps to prevent cavities. Sleepiness is not usually a problem since the medicine can be taken before bed time. If a child becomes constipated, contact your doctor so that this can be corrected.

Other less common effects include blurred vision, trouble starting to urinate, flushing of the skin (feeling hot or having part of the body get very red), increased sweating, bad breath, vivid dreams and nausea. These problems are more common in adolescents and adults. Occasionally the medication causes postural hypotension (feeling dizzy when standing up quickly). Sitting down and getting up slowly is the solution to this problem.

Very rarely a person taking the tricyclic antidepressants will have a change in heart rate with the heart going faster than usual. Stopping the medication makes this problem go away. It may be possible to carefully try a different tricyclic without this problem recurring. Other very rare problems include skin rashes and unusual movements of the tongue or large muscles. These also go away when the medication is stopped. Serious heart problems have been reported when overdoses of antidepressants have been taken.

Are There Any Medications That Should Not Be Taken With The Tricyclics?

The tricyclics should be given with care with painkillers and antihistamines (often found in cold medicines). Tricyclics and these medications both cause sedation (feeling tired) and slowed response time. Activities that demand alertness, such as driving, may need to be avoided when these medications are taken at the same time. The tricyclic antidepressants potentiate the effects of alcohol. When taking this medication it is best to refrain from using alcoholic beverages. Some children cold and cough preparations contain significant amounts of alcohol. Read the labels carefully of non-prescription medications given to children on tricyclics.

Can The Tricyclics Be Dangerous?

Yes, these medications can be harmful if they are not taken as directed by your doctor. Be sure to keep this medicine (all medicines) in a locked or safe place out of the reach of children. The tricyclics are especially dangerous and can be lethal if large amounts are accidentally taken by children or adults. Be sure to contact poison control or your doctor at once if this should happen.

10

Comparison of Medications Used to Treat Attention Deficit Disorders

LENGTH OF ACTION	CONTROLLED SUBSTANCE?	POTENTIAL FOR ABUSE?	ADVANTAGES	DISADVANTAGES & SIDE EFFECTS
Methylphenidate (Ritalin) tablet: 3–4 hrs yes yes *Methylphenidate (Ritalin SR) slow release:* 6–8 hrs yes yes *Dextroamphetamine (Dexadrine) tablet or elixir:* 4–6 hrs yes yes *Dextroamphetamine (Dexadrine) spansule:* 8–12 hrs yes yes			1. Works right away.	1. Some loss of appetite. 2. Must mail script each month. 3. Variable duration of action.
Pemoline (Cylert): 12–18 hrs no no			1. Taken daily in mornings only. 2. Prescription can be refilled by phone. Pharmacy can dispense only one month at a time. 3. Comes in chewable tablet. Regular tablet can also be chewed.	1. Decrease in appetite. 2. May cause trouble getting to sleep. 3. Takes 1 to 4 weeks to work. 4. Start and stop gradually. 5. Rare cause of changes in liver enzymes.
Tricyclics: 8–24 hrs no no			1. Take daily dose at night. 2. Prescription can be called in for six months. Refilled for one month. 3. May also help bedwetting and some mood problems.	1. Dry mouth constipation, blurry vision, & tiredness in some children. 2. May take 2–6 weeks to see benefit.

11

Information About Lithium

Lithium is one of several medications that is used to prevent mood swings in people with affective disorders. The FDA (Food and Drug Administration) approved its use for treating manic episodes in 1970 and for maintenance therapy in severe affective disorders in 1974. Lithium has been used with varying success to treat older children with a variety of mood or behavioral problems. At present, the manufacturers of lithium have not completed the extensive clinical trials that are necessary for lithium to be approved by the FDA for use in children under twelve years of age. Children who have severe mood disorders that are only partly responsive to other medications have been shown to respond to lithium in clinical trials. Generally these children have a family history of manic depressive or affective disorder.

How Is Lithium Given?

Lithium is taken by mouth two or three times a day. It comes as a tablet, a slow-release tablet, a capsule and an elixir and is available in several different strengths.

Adverse side effects are a common problem with lithium therapy and are discussed in more detail below. Very serious reactions can occur when too much medication is taken. It is essential to closely monitor children and adults while they take this medicine.

Are There Any People Who Should Not Take Lithium?

Pregnant women or women who are trying to get pregnant should not take lithium. Lithium causes severe cardiac malformations in unborn babies and should not be used during the first months of pregnancy unless the potential benefits outweigh the possible hazards. Most physicians discourage mothers who are on lithium from breastfeeding because the lithium is excreted in significant amounts in breast milk. People with heart, kidney, thyroid or other unstable medical illness must be followed with great care if they are taking this medication.

What Are The Side Effects Of Lithium?

Most children tolerate lithium without any problem from side effects. The more common side effects are drowsiness, slight tremor of the hands, increased urination, thirst, weight gain, nausea and diarrhea. The concentration of lithium in the blood is dependent on salt and water balance in the body. It is important that people on lithium maintain a normal diet and a regular salt and water intake.

Rarely, there may be a problem with the function of the kidneys or thyroid gland. Blood tests are recommended at regular intervals to monitor kidney and thyroid function. Lithium also causes or worsens acne in adolescents.

What Are The Effects of Too Much Lithium?

Lithium has a relatively narrow theraputic range (0.6 mEq/L to 1.2 mEq/L). Blood levels are necessary to monitor the dose of lithium, particularly in children. When the concentration of lithium increases above the theraputic range, vomiting, diarrhea, muscle weakness and lack of coordination may occur. At very toxic doses, giddiness, blurred vision, ringing of the ears and severe lack of coordination may be seen.

Are There Any Medications That Shouldn't Be Taken With Lithium?

Various medications can interact with lithium. In some instances this will cause a change in the metabolism of one or both medications. Adverse reactions may be seen when lithium is combined with other medications. Some of these medications that interact with lithium include tegretol, theophylline, thiazide diuretics and potassium iodide. The non-steroidal antiinflammatory agents (Motrin, Advil, Nalfon, etc.) and medications used to treat stomach ulcers (Tagamet, Zantac, etc.) may cause an increase in the plasma lithium level. Be sure your physician is aware of all medications you take. Lithium levels should be obtained at regular intervals.

SUGGESTED READING ABOUT LITHIUM

Bohn, J. and J. Jefferson. *Lithium And Manic Depression, A Guide.* Lithium Information Center, University of Wisconsin, Madison, Wisc., 4th revision. 1987. 33 Pages. Paperback. $3.50 (includes mailing costs). May be obtained from the Lithium Information Center, Department of Psychiatry, University of Wisc. Center for Health Sciences, 600 Highland Avenue, Madison, Wisconsin, 53792. A brief but excellent primer on the use of lithium in the treatment of manic-depressive disorder.

12

Self-Esteem

Children with attention, behavior and learning problems frequently have problems with self-esteem and confidence. Parents and teachers find themselves frustrated trying to help these children appreciate their strengths and feel good about themselves. Our technical society makes this task more difficult. Intelligence and academic achievement are highly valued. Children with special needs struggle in school, rarely understand the nature of their difficulty and are usually brighter than they think they are. Public and private schools with limited funds attempt to provide some form of individualized instruction for children with special needs. Children with learning and behavioral problems feel out of place in the classroom. They don't fit in with their peers. They don't learn or "test" well in the classroom. Parents who have struggled "in the dark" are relieved to learn more about the nature and treatment of their child's problems. Children may not have the same positive response when presented with a diagnosis and treatment plan. It is important to present this information in a way that it can be used constructively by the child.

How Does A Parent Tell The Child About Their Problem?

Many children are unaware of their own attention or mood problems. They understand the implications of poor report cards or what it means to be treated differently in the classroom. Most of us find it unpleasant to listen when other people discuss our problems. Children will usually deny that they have a problem in order to "save face." If it is necessary to discuss the problems a young child is having with a friend or professional, be sure to find a place where the child can read or play so that these matters can be discussed in private. An older child should be given the option of participating in the discussion. If an older child is present during the review of information, be sure that the discussion is balanced with positive and negative comments.

It is helpful to think of a child's learning or behavioral problems within the context of the entire family. Although the disability may appear to be only the child's, the problem actually belongs to the entire family. Treatment in the broad sense must begin within the family. This family approach is helpful to the child with the identified problem. When the problem can be

shared even to a small degree by the entire family, it is easier for the identified child. When a child is about to be evaluated, explain that the family
or parents need to find better solutions to improve the quality of life at home
and at school. It is truthful to admit that the adults have run out of good
ideas and need the help of an expert. The problems then belong to more
than one family member and the child is often more willing to cooperate
in exploring solutions.

Robert has been struggling in third grade because of long-stand-
ing attention problems. His teacher suspects he has an attention
deficit disorder. His parents have made an appointment for an eval-
uation. The night before the evaluation appointment, Robert's mother
finds a quiet place to talk to him.

She says, "Robert, you know that your teacher, Mrs. Peters, and
I have talked to each other a lot this year. Last year, your teacher
and I talked a lot too. Your teachers have always told me that you
have such interesting ideas and that you really do understand new
things quickly. They know it takes you a long time to finish your
work at school and that you bring a lot of home work home at night.
Do you know what I'm talking about?"

Robert responds sadly; "Yeah, I always have more home work
to do than anyone else. I never have any time to play at night."

His mother continues; "Robert, can you think of some of the
other things that happen in your classroom that are frustrating to
you?"

"Sure, I always have my name on the board for talking or getting
into trouble. No one else in my class has to have notes go home every
day. I really hate that." Robert responds.

"That must be very frustrating. I know you have tried hard to
keep your name off the board and to get your work done. Your teachers
have tried to think of ways to help too. Mrs. Peters thinks that there
may be a way to help so that you can get your work done more quickly
and be in better control of yourself. Tomorrow, we are going to talk
with a doctor who we think may be able to give us some help making
school go more smoothly. She helps children who are having this kind
of frustration in school. She will examine you and talk with you. Then
she'll talk with us and ask us lots of questions. We'll probably ask
her questions too. As soon as the appointment is over, we'll drive
you back to school. Let me know if you have any questions about the
visit before we go."

How Can A Parent Or Teacher Help A Child Develop Positive Self-esteem?

Parents and teachers can help children with special needs develop
positive self-esteem. A first step is to reexamine your own values and prior-

ities. Teaching these values through stories, games, directions and descriptions as well as in your actions, is the next step.

First, help your child learn the value and uniqueness of each and every human being. We are unique because of our strengths and our weaknesses, our likes and our dislikes. The strengths and weaknesses of some people seem to stand out. You must get to know other people well before you learn about their abilities or their problems. The strengths and positive attributes people have may include such diverse things as: playing a musical instrument well, physical strength, inventiveness and creativity, listening well, remembering well, handling animals carefully and easily, kindness and sensitivity to the feelings of other people, getting along well with other people, liking being alone, reading well, patience and tolerance for young children, and having a cheerful disposition. Some examples of weaknesses are: forgetting easily, poor coordination, feeling uncomfortable around other people, getting angry easily, trouble with writing or drawing, slow reading, weak muscles, being anxious or fearful, or being rigid and opinionated. There are times when the same characteristic may be seen as a strength and at other times as a weakness. Children with attention, learning and behavior problems are usually aware of their negative attributes. It may be harder for them, and more important for them, to be aware of their abilities and strengths.

Second, help your child to understand that life is better seen as a cooperative venture where everyone works together toward a goal, rather than a race where only one person can be the best. Making your best effort, learning what your strengths are and making good use of them, learning how to overcome your areas of weakness, making life a little better for someone else—this is success. Feeling good about yourself must first come from inside of you, from liking who you are and accepting the positive and the negative sides of you, and from being tolerant and accepting of the same in other people.

Help your child learn that as children and adults grow and mature, they are capable of doing harder, more difficult tasks. Some of our best abilities may not develop until we are teenagers or adults. Children may be unaware of how important time, motivation and hard work are to success. A task that is difficult for your child at this age may be much easier in a year or two. Give your child examples of adults and children who have worked hard to overcome disabilities and handicaps or were "late bloomers."

Help your child identify her own strengths and successful strategies for managing difficult tasks.

> *Patty's mother sees Patty playing gently with the neighbor's kitten. "Patty, you are patting the kitten so gently. You seem to know just how to make the kitten happy."*

Then help her be aware when she tackles a difficult task successfully.

"I've watched you spend extra effort to copy that picture very carefully. When you spend extra time and effort like that, your pictures are neat and colorful."

"Robert, you took the time last night to organize your school work for today. That gave you extra time to eat breakfast and I really liked not having to remind you to get your books ready for school this morning."

Explain that many people work hard to make life better for other people. We all depend on other people to make our lives more comfortable and to stay healthy. Help comes in many ways. Glasses and contact lenses enable people with poor eyesight to see normally. Typewriters and computers make writing easier for many people. Researchers continue to discover medicines that help children who have various medical problems feel better. Doctors can help children who have trouble concentrating or who get very angry or sad. Children and grown-ups like being healthy. Most of us would rather not have to have tests, see a doctor regularly, work with a tutor or take medication. There are times when each of us needs to work with another person or several other people to solve a problem.

Listen to your child's concerns and respect his feelings. Tell your child that you love him. Tell him, with no "strings attached", that you are glad he is a member of your family and that he is unique and special. Children have a hard time understanding that the love of a parent for a child remains constant. When parents get angry, they must give clear messages to the child that their anger is at the child's specific behavior not at the child. Certain times will be especially stressful for both your child and your family. Children need parents who can listen without judging, support and love them even when life is unfair or harsh.

SUGGESTED READING ON BUILDING
SELF-ESTEEM IN CHILDREN

Clark, Jean Illsley. *Self-Esteem: A Family Affair.* New York: Harper and Row, 1978, 280 pages, paperback, $9.95. Very useful book offering parents ideas and tools for parenting that provide positive self-esteem for children of different ages.

13

Management Techniques

Children with attention deficits, learning and behavioral problems can be very challenging. Their problems with concentration, poor impulse control, distractibility and frequent hyperactivity make daily management a difficult struggle. Parents and school personnel want to do as much as they can to make life at home and school go smoothly. These children need more than the usual love, patience, consistency and firm guidance.

The techniques below appear simple and easy when read. Putting them into practice takes time, self-examination, patience and hard work. Focus on one technique at a time and think about how it affects the various problems you want to change. Refer to the ideas below when you need help in handling a stubborn or difficult situation. When you get stuck and can't resolve a problem behavior, get help from a professional who specializes in working with children.

1. Think positively about discipline. Discipline is the process of teaching a child the rules of behavior and how the child's behavior affects other people. It is the gradual learning of limits and of the rights of other people. It is not punishment. It is part of the process by which our children develop a sense of meaning and purpose for living. Children need limits and structure to develop self confidence, self respect and respect for others. Part of growing up involves learning to be responsible for our actions, knowing our own limits and acting in ways that cause no harm to ourselves and other people. Children need to have limits and structure in their lives geared to their age, developmental stage and maturity. Eventually your children should develop controls within themselves and be able to postpone immediate desires in the interest of long term satisfactions and achievements. Remember that children learn by example. Hitting, even for severe misbehavior, teaches children that there are certain times when hitting is permissible.

2. Tell your child with words and with a hug at least once a day that you love him and that you are glad that he is a part of your family. Never attach conditions to these messages.

3. Notice and praise your child's good behavior. Describe what it is about the good behavior that you like. Children, especially difficult children, need lots of positive reinforcement.

Kathy asks nicely, "Mommy, would you help me make my lunch for school?"

Mother responds, delighted that Kathy has not whined, "Kathy, you asked that question in a calm voice. I really like doing things for you when you ask with that voice. I'd be glad to help you."

4. Use "descriptive" praise. Describe what your child has done and how it made you feel.

"Your picture has such bright blues, reds and interesting colors in it. That looks like a rainbow to me. Bright colors cheer me up!"

Try to avoid judgemental comments like "It's a beautiful picture." "You're such a good painter." Children, and adults too, are aware of their shortcomings and discount this kind of compliment, even though it may be well-intended. Children with attention and learning problems are especially sensitive about their limitations. Praise that does not judge the child's character or evaluate his personality makes it safe for the child to make mistakes without fear and to try again.

5. Children with behavior and learning problems are vulnerable and their feelings can be hurt easily. Never belittle or humiliate your child. Try not to compare your child's behavior or progress to other children. Instead, tell your child what she needs to do to behave appropriately.

6. Keep instructions simple. Children with attention problems have trouble remembering complicated instructions. Give your child one instruction and when that task is finished give the second instruction. Go through the task yourself to get a better idea of the steps involved. Have your child repeat back to you the instructions you want him to follow. Remember that your child can't control his distractibility without enormous effort. He can only keep one instruction in his head at a time. For older children, lists or written directions can be helpful.

7. Keep instructions clear. Most children will understand what you mean if you ask them to follow a somewhat generalized direction. Children with attention and learning problems need clear and specific directions. An unclear message is:

"Your father is sleeping upstairs and he is really tired. Please try not to wake him."

The same direction is clearer when given this way:

"Your father is sleeping upstairs and is really tired. Stay away from his room. If you need to go near his room, whisper quietly and wait until you are downstairs to talk."

Your child now understands that there is a connection between making noise and waking up his father.

8. Talk positively to your children. Tell your child what it is you want her to do, rather than what she shouldn't do. If your child is yelling, say, "Use a quiet voice," rather than "Stop all that yelling." If your child is throwing toys, say, "The toys belong on the floor where they can be played with," rather than "Stop throwing those toys."

9. Be sure you have your child's full attention before you ask him to do something. Children with attention problems often do not paying attention to what you want them to pay attention to. Stop your child, be sure you have eye contact and then give instructions. This is much more effective than yelling a direction up the stairs. When you have to repeat a direction, say it each time as though it were the first time. Have your child repeat the instruction back to you.

10. Use a hand signal to help your child pay attention. When your child needs to look directly at you and pay attention to what you have to say, bring your index finger up to your forehead. Teach your child that when you do this it means; "Time for eye contact! Pay attention! This is important!"

11. Give your child extra help in organizing tasks. He can and should do the job himself but needs added direction. Often asking your child to stop and think what he is doing now and what he should do next will help him to refocus and complete the next part of the job. Expect to help your child get upstairs, out of dirty clothes, into pajamas and into the bathroom to brush teeth and to bathe. Often just going along and providing a verbal reminder like, "what comes next," will help. For example:

> *"It's time to go upstairs now. What needs to go upstairs with you for bedtime? Now that your P.J.'s are on, what else do you need to do before we read a story? Now that your teeth are brushed, what is the next thing you need to do? Stop and think a minute, what has to be done for school tomorrow."*

Use check lists for tasks that are part of your child's routine. Teach your child to stop and think if she has everything she needs before leaving the house in the morning. Help your child organize her belongings and home work before going to bed at night so there is less to do in the morning when there is less time.

12. Provide sequencing for your child. Give the overview first and then break down instructions into simple tasks. Give one or two directions at a time. Then have her come back to you for additional instructions. Children with ADD are slower in developing skills for organizing and need help until they are much older. Help older children make up lists for tasks they need

to do each day. Help your child to remember to use the lists in school. For example, to help remember what to bring home at the end of the school day, tape a check list on the inside of her school locker. Eventually she will use these organizing techniques and make use of them in other parts of her life.

13. Help your child increase his attention span and lessen distractibility. Gently remind your child to stay with one thought when talking or one task when it has been started. When she becomes distracted, remind her of what she started talking about and request that she finish the thought or the activity before starting off in another direction.

14. Try to provide a routine at home. Times of stress (for example: getting children ready for school, meal time and bed time) will be easier if there is a regular routine.

15. Be consistent when you discipline. Give your child one warning and then follow through with established consequences. Consequences for inappropriate behavior should be immediate and brief. Do not threaten a punishment if you know you won't follow through with the consequences.

16. Pay attention to the amount of disorder, noise and distraction around the house. Choose quiet music when everyone is tired and edgy. Turn off the TV if it is adding to the noise and confusion. Move the TV into a quiet room. When it feels like there are too many toys around the house for your child (or you) to manage, put some away in the attic or closet for a while and rotate them. Make cleaning up easy with labeled bins and boxes for toys. Try using a noisy timer to help speed up your child's clean-up chores.

17. Provide frequent opportunities for your child to let off physical energy. Many children with ADD have extra energy to burn and become very frustrated when they are confined. This is particularly important in the winter.

18. Make sure you plan enough time for various tasks. Nothing is worse hurrying a child who has trouble complying because there is too little time. Children with attention and behavior problems don't understand about being on time. They think and act only in the present. Use a digital clock to let your child know how long you expect a task to take.

> *Daniel, you need to get dressed and finish in the bathroom by 7:30 AM. At 7:30 AM you need to come into the kitchen for breakfast.*

19. Help provide social settings in which your child will be successful. Children with attention problems are often socially immature. They need help organizing successful encounters with other children. Keep play situations short and simple with just one playmate until you are sure your child can handle the situation well. Expect to be around to supervise and head off

difficult situations. Provide activities that both children are likely to enjoy rather than letting them disagree about what to do. This is easier to do with younger children. Your child will learn and have success with other children with your help. Be patient. As your child gets older, take advantage of organized activities such as Boy Scouts, Girl Scouts, church groups and 4-H programs. One parent may need to be present to supervise if your child's behavior is very disruptive.

20. Practice social skills with your child (ages 4 to 8). Let your child rehearse with you what he will say when calling on the phone to invite another child to play. When you and your child are riding in the car together, suggest that he play a game with you. Give him a pretend situation and ask him to tell you what he would do if he were in that situation. Talk about his response and ask if he has any other ideas. Try to gently guide your child into more appropriate and polite social responses. Encourage your child to watch television "family shows" that have parents interacting in a positive way with children. Watch these programs with your child and discuss the situations with him.

21. When giving instructions or showing your child how to do something, use as many of her senses (hearing, seeing, touching, moving) as you can. Try to identify the ways your child learns best. Some children are better visual learners and other children learn better by hearing. Many children need to see and hear together to learn best. Touching an object or moving it around may be helpful to other children.

22. If your child has trouble with temper tantrums, find a quiet, boring, safe place in the house (the bathroom or stairs) where she can cool down without too much stimulation (toys, bright colors, lots of noise) and can't hurt herself or the furniture. If possible, do not use her bedroom for this. Send or take her there when she misbehaves and tell her she should come back when she is able to act in a mature way. Return her to the quiet place if she continues to misbehave. Be sure to act quickly with time-outs. Give your child one warning and with the next behavior, take her for a time-out. Once you take your child for a time-out, do not talk, yell or argue with her until the time-out is over except to remind her of the time-out rules.

23. Consider having a regular "special" time for each child in your family. Start with five or ten minutes several times a week. The child may choose the activity (with parental consent) for "special" time. Developing a dependable, regular time to be with each child helps communication and sharing of feelings. Try to make some of the "special" time at night. Children will often talk about important things that happened during the day if given a quiet "cuddle" time before bed.

24. Try to keep your sense of humor. Many difficult situations are better handled with a touch of humor rather than anger.

25. Keep your voice down and your anger under control. This is one of the most difficult things for parents to do and is especially difficult when your child has special needs. Be sure you get enough sleep. A tired parent is usually short on patience.

26. Child-proof your home with special care. Children with attention problems are accident-prone and touch things they shouldn't. Provide extra supervision to keep your child safe. Watch for potential danger around the house. Put away any harmful articles (hammer, saw, nails, matches, knives, etc.) after they are used. Lock up medicines and other dangerous items.

27. Children with attention problems are impulsive and have a hard time waiting their turn. Your child may talk without being aware that someone else is talking. Remind him to listen first before talking, that you are talking to someone else and will talk with him when you are finished. Try to be consistent and at the same time remember that because of his impulsivity, it will take him greater effort to control his behavior.

28. Limit the number of decisions your child has to make. Make her choices simple. Many children are overwhelmed by a question like "What do you want for lunch?" They can better handle the choice between a peanut butter sandwich and cottage cheese. For other children, even the choice between two items is too much. Be direct and simple. "Lunch is ready." Without discussing that tuesday night is the night for hair washing, bring your child into the bathroom and start her bath.

29. Discuss your concerns about your child with a friend or professional out of the hearing of the child. If you must discuss your child's problems in his presence, be sure to phrase your words carefully so that the child does not feel embarrassed or humiliated.

30. Don't "bite off more that you can chew." Choose one or two behaviors to work on at a time. Change comes gradually and is easier on you and your child if it is done in small, focused steps. Feel good when you have taken each small step.

31. Limit the amount of time you and your children watch television. Try to turn on the radio or record player instead of the TV. Read to your child on a regular basis and encourage your child to read alone. Often a parent turns on the TV to watch a show he or she likes. The TV then stays on all afternoon or all evening. If you have a VCR, use it to provide educational TV at times that are appropriate for your child.

32. Help provide a quiet area for your child for doing home work. Children with attention and learning problems need a clean surface with minimal distractions. Your child may not be able to finish his home work in a reasonable amount of time unless a parent is in the room to keep him on task.

If you need to do this, try to be as quiet and unobtrusive as possible. Read or work on a "desk type" task while you supervise your child's home work. Your child should do the work himself with your supervision.

33. Talk positively about your spouse and about your work (raising children is hard and important work, too). When children hear their parents belittle each other or talk in a negative way about each other's work, children pick up the same attitudes and see their parents work efforts as less valuable. Parents may be negative unintentionally. For example: "I can't wait for the weekend" or "Why didn't you get this house cleaned up today?" may be understood by the child as "I really don't like going to work and would rather not do it" or "You aren't doing a very good job keeping the house clean." A healthier message would be: "I really like my work and I work hard when I'm there. I also look forward to a chance to relax and choose what I do when the weekends come," and "You must have had a lot to do today. Were you planning to straighten up the house tomorrow or would you like us to help with that tonight?"

34. Talk over problem areas with your spouse (and other supportive friends). Parents are more effective with their children if they work together using the same techniques. If other people (including your spouse) approach a problem differently and have better results with it, find out why. Sometimes just re-evaluating the situation can give you new insights and ideas. Seek the advice of a professional if you and your spouse are unable to agree about the nature of your child's problems. Have a regularly planned time to enjoy being with your spouse. "Special" time is as important for adults as it is for children.

35. Stay in touch with the physician who is managing medications used to treat your child's behavior and medical problems. Medications can help with specific problems but at times can make behavior worse. Your physician can best help you manage your child's medical needs when you provide accurate information and keep in touch as he or she directs.

36. Keep in close touch with your child's teacher and school. Talk about the problems you have at home with your child's teacher and the techniques you are using to manage them. Ask the teacher what management strategies work in the classroom. Try to be consistent at home and at school. Inform your child's teacher or school nurse of any changes in medication. Suggest to the teacher that you jointly start a notebook with observations and comments. The book should go back and forth from home to school weekly or daily. Bring this notebook in when your child sees the doctor. Any changes of medication or concerns can be shared easily.

37. Share materials with your child's teacher and doctor that have helped you understand your child and your child's problems. Many well-meaning

professionals and educators (and family members too) do not understand why these children have trouble with concentration, distractibility, impulse control, behavior and learning. They assume the child is misbehaving deliberately. Other people blame parents for not bringing up their children "right." Understanding the problem is the first step in dealing with it effectively. Teachers may not be aware of a child's problems even though the school has an extensive file on the child. Some teachers prefer to experience the child without the bias of previous information. It may be necessary each fall to arrange a conference with your child's teacher to review the concerns you have about your child.

38. Remember that at times, parenting is a demanding and difficult task even for skilled parents. Contrary to popular belief, answers to difficult problems do not come "naturally" for most parents. There are few places in our educational system where young adults learn about parenting and child development. It is especially difficult to parent children with behavioral, learning and attention problems. Many parents find that they need to learn more and become more skilled at management. Help may come from friends, professionals, parent groups and from written material.

SUGGESTED READINGS ON MANAGEMENT AND DISCIPLINE

Turecki, Stanley. *The Difficult Child.* New York: Bantum. 1985. Hardcover. about $16.00. Excellent book about the temperamental differences of difficult children. Very useful information about handling various kinds of discipline and behavior problems.

Wycoff, Jerry and B. Unell. *Discipline Without Shouting Or Spanking.* Meadowbrook Press, 1984, paperback, about $6.00. This book offers effective, practical, nonviolent options for correcting the most common behavior problems of preschoolers. This easy-to-use text is in a first-aid manual format.

Canter, Lee. *Assertive Discipline For Parents.* New York: Harper and Row. 1985. 122 pages. paperback. $7.95. This book gives straight-forward, step by step approaches to solving everyday behavior problems. A systematic program designed to enable parents to take charge of their children's behavior in a firm, consistent and loving manner is described.

14

Resources

PERIODICALS

The Exceptional Parent
605 Commonwealth Avenue
Boston, Massachusetts, 02215
   Excellent journal for parents of children with developmental disabilities and special needs. Issued eight times a year. Subscription costs about $16.00 per year.

NATIONAL AND STATE ORGANIZATIONS

Annual Directory of Organizations
Published by *The Exceptional Parent* Magazine in each September issue
605 Commonwealth Avenue.
Boston, Massachusetts, 02215
   Extensive directory of national and regional organizations and parent groups providing information and advocacy about disorders that affect children.

Association for Children with Learning Disabilities (ACLD)
4156 Library Road
Pittsburgh, PA., 15234
   Non-profit national organization devoted to defining and finding solutions for the broad spectrum of learning problems. It is supported by membership dues, grants and sale of publications. A newsletter is published every other month and covers developments in the field of learning disorders. The organization sponsors national and state conferences and has a reference library of over 500 publications, most of which are available for sale. Most states have chapters of the ACLD.

Wisconsin Association for Children with Learning Disabilities (WACLD)
5218 Century Avenue
Middleton, Wisconsin, 53562
  Non-profit state organization (many areas have a local or state chapter of the ACLD) that provides educational material, resources, parent support groups, conferences, speakers, a newsletter and other services for Wisconsin families.

Orton Dyslexia Society
724 York Road
Baltimore, Maryland, 21204
  This national organization provides information and support for professionals as well as adults and children and their parents with dyslexia.

Wisconsin Association for Hyperactive Children (WAHC)
P.O. Box 1477
Milwaukee, Wisconsin, 53201
  The WAHC is a non-profit educational organization for parents and professionals in Wisconsin interested in children with attention deficit disorders. The group meets monthly in Milwaukee and also sponsors parent group meetings in Waukesha, Germantown, Kenosha, Wisconsin. Membership dues ($15.00) provide use of WAHC library, WAHC newsletter, an information packet, membership in WACLD and ACLD. Many states have similar associations.

Alliance for the Mentally Ill, Inc. (AMI)
1901 North Fort Myer Drive, Suite 500
Arlington, Va. 22209-1607
(703) 524-7600
  National organization for adults with psychiatric disorders and their families. This organization began with the Wisconsin chapter and has been a very strong advocate for the rights and services of the mentally ill.

Alliance for the Mentally Ill of Wisconsin, Inc. (AMI)
1245 East Washington Avenue., Suite 212
Madison, Wisconsin, 53703
(608) 257-5888

Wisconsin chapter of AMI
PEP (Parent Education Project)
United Cerebral Palsey of Southeastern Wisconsin, Inc.
230 West Wells Street, Suite 502
Milwaukee, Wisconsin, 53203
(414) 272-4500
    PEP is a coalition of parent groups and agencies whose purpose is to help parents of children with disabilities to work with the schools. PEP is for parents of children ages 3-21 who live in Wisconsin. The groups that participate in PEP believe that well-informed parents are the best advocates for their children. PEP is funded thru a grant that is administered by United Cerebral Palsy of Southeastern Wisconsin, Inc.

National Neurofibromatosis Foundation
70 West 40th Street
New York, New York, 10018

National Tuberous Sclerosis Association, Inc.
P.O. Box 159
Laguna Beach, California, 92652

Tourette Syndrome Association
41-02 Bell Boulevard
Bayside, New York, 11361

The Fragile X Foundation
P.O. Box 3300233
Denver, Colorado, 80203

ABOUT THE AUTHOR

Dr. Coleman received her undergraduate degree from Wheaton College, Norton, Massachusetts and her medical degree from The Medical College of Pennsylvania. Her internship and residency in pediatrics were completed at St. Christopher's Hospital for Children in Philadelphia, Pennsylvania. After residency, her training included fellowships in Pediatric Hematology and Behavioral Pediatrics at the University of Wisconsin Hospital and Clinics, Madison.

Dr. Coleman has worked as a behavioral and general pediatrician at the Jackson Clinic since 1978. She specializes in the evaluation, medical treatment and coordination of care of children with attention deficit disorders and behavioral problems. Dr. Coleman is a strong advocate for children with developmental, learning and behavioral problems. She writes educational materials for parents of healthy children at the Jackson Clinic and also speaks on various topics for school districts, parent groups, conferences and agencies. She is married and has three children.

2115 Chadbourne Avenue
Madison, Wisconsin
53705

ORDER FORM

Please send me the following:

Attention Deficit Disorders and Hyperactivity
5th Edition–Soft Cover

————
    1 to 9 books $ 6.00 each
    10 to 19 books $ 5.25 each
    20 or more books $ 4.50 each $ ————

Attention Deficit Disorders and Hyperactivity
5th Edition–Hard Cover

————
    1 to 4 books $11.95 each
    5 or more books   8.00 each $ ————

....

                                      Total cost of books $ ————

Shipping and handling costs: 1 book $1.50
                              2 to 4 books   2.00
                              5 to 10 books   3.50
                              11 to 19 books   4.50 $ ————

....

Subtotal for books, shipping and handling $ ————

Wisconsin residents please add 5% sales tax on
books, shipping and handling costs $ ————

....

                                       Total enclosed $ ————

Make checks payable to: Calliope Books

Send to:

      Name ——————————————————————————

   Address ——————————————————————————

                ——————————————— Zip ————————